Stickman's Battles

Stickman's Battles

The Growing Believer Confronts the Seven Deadly Sins

Terry Ewing

VMI Publishers • Sisters, Oregon

Published by
VMI Publishers
Sisters, Oregon
www.vmipubishers.com

ISBN 13: 978-1-933204-80-2
ISBN 10: 1-933204-80-X

Library of Congress: 2009921869

Printed in the USA

Cover design by Joe Bailen

Table of Contents

Introduction

The stickman on the cover of this book may look strange to you. He is covered in the armor of God, yet he remains a skinny, weak, stickman. Don't we suppose that the Christian covered in the armor of God should look more like a strong, capable warrior?

In order for you to benefit from this book, we need to start with the same presupposition. I believe that the strongest we can possibly be is when we acknowledge our weaknesses and cling to the armor of God. It is in trusting God, not ourselves, that we can humbly receive all the healing, love, and growth that He has for us. So, let's begin with this assumption; that you are a stickman in need of healing and growth.

If I were to ask those who know you best to tell me about how you have grown in Christ-likeness over the last three to seven years, what would they tell me? Would they be able to name a virtue that they observe developing in you? Would they be able to name vices that Christ has overcome in you?

Please don't confuse these questions with those concerning new truths, trials endured, or ministries performed. You may have gone through any number of changes in theology, circumstances, and relationships without being changed in character. You could develop insights, commit to ministries, perform spiritual disciplines, change jobs, get married, and get in shape without becoming more Christ-like.

You may ask, "If not by these outward signs, how is anyone to know whether I've grown or not?" While only God can see an individual's heart, he has called us to encourage each other in faith and purity. This study of the Seven Deadly Sins can serve as a life-time tool in identifying, sharing, and encouraging each other in our unique struggles with our carnal nature.

I began my study of the Seven Deadly Sins years ago as an addendum to my teaching on forgiveness. As presented in chapter 7 of *Stickman Theology*, I believe that forgiveness does not mean that we overlook an offense to us in order to be reconciled, but that we are willing to be reconciled to our offender if they are humble and accountable. A part of reconciliation is an identification of and accountability for our sin motivations. I studied the Seven Deadly Sins as a tool created by the early Christian Church fathers for identifying our sin motivations. As I taught on forgiveness I found that people were looking for appropriate ways to discuss sin motivations openly and honestly, yet without rejection or condemnation.

The first time I preached a series of sermons on sin motivations for my home church, I was concerned that the topic would not attract or hold attendance. I was surprised to see that the topic attracted a larger than average attendance and that the attendance increased over the course of the eight weeks that I preached the series. I was told how valuable it was for people to have a means of diagnosing their predominant sin motivations and how much freedom it gave them in relating to each other as "struggling, striving, growing Christians" (a capsule statement of my understanding of the nature of discipleship).

A young man who attended those services had begun an informal Friday night service for young adults (twenty- to thirty-two-year-olds). He asked if I would teach the series again for this group. Again, I was skeptical that this topic would hold or draw young people. And, again, I was proven wrong. The first night eighteen young people were present (which was their average group). Before the series ended we were averaging thirty-two to thirty-four. These young people were eager to understand themselves and their temptations. After a time of worship and the forty-minute teaching, the young people would ask questions for another hour each week.

Meanwhile, in my counseling practice, people were setting aside their resistances and embracing their emotional and relational dysfunctions when their dysfunctions were related by me to sin motivations. I found that Christians really do want to identify the spiritual nature of their struggles and learn how to trust the Holy Spirit in their fight with sin. People want to be able to repent (turn away from) their sin motivations, not just their sinful behavior. Each sin motivation is unique and requires a unique response of the Holy Spirit and application of the promises of God. Sin serves a purpose in our lives. Sin is a means (temporary and destructive though it may be) of trying to meet legitimate needs in our lives. Unless we can identify those needs, we are not able to seek God's provision for them. By naming our sin motivations, we are able to identify the legitimate needs behind them and be open to receiving God's provision for them.

Therefore, this study is not a series of denunciations of particular sinful actions and illustrations of their destructiveness, but a life-giving study of what God has provided for us to turn toward to meet needs that the sin we're turning from has previously met!

I have come to realize that the dynamic of identifying sin motivations in order to understand our legitimate needs and present them to God is one the Church is thirsty for. This study promotes the principle that every local church is intended by God to be a safe place where Christians will struggle, strive, and grow together. I have found that few Christians have ever experienced such an honest, transparent, and safe community. Yet, we all hunger for it; the community of the humble, the community of the encouragers, the community of the kindred spirits, the community of those who are bold and courageous enough to identify their sin, their motivations, and their needs.

It is my sincere prayer that you are part of such a fellowship or soon will be. This curriculum is meant to be studied in the context of a small group with intimate sharing. If you are now committed to going through this study with such a group, let me offer you encouragement and a warning.

First, the encouragement: be prepared to give and receive love intimately! Stretch beyond your comfort zone. Let there be no secrets and no shame. Let there be no theological defensiveness and no condemnations. Let there be no inhibitions against crying, laughing, embarrassment, anger, or fears: acknowledge them as they come and represent them to the group.

No one can honestly evaluate their sin motivations without a willingness to shed light in the dark corners of their feelings, attitudes, and behaviors. This course will bring understanding of yourself, others, and God, but that is not its primary purpose. This course is intended to guide you in your fellowship with others as you witness each other struggling, striving, and growing!

Now, the warning: if you cannot trust those within your group to not condemn you for your struggles or to participate transparently themselves, you have two options. One, sit quietly and observe your group's dynamics for a couple of weeks. They may be able to earn your trust and help overcome your inhibitions. You need to understand that each of your group members will also be risking a lot by fully participating in this group. Several may feel the same way you do. Be patient, and persevere. Let God move gently among you. There are blessings God intends for you that come only through intimate fellowship. Give it a chance. Or, two, you may feel like you can't trust everyone in your group to keep confidences and participate honestly in the work of this curriculum. And your feelings may be accurate. There really may be an unsafe person or two in your group. At this point you should prayerfully consider raising these concerns within your group or withdrawing from this study until you can identify a group you believe will be safer for you. I'm sorry to even have to offer this warning, but experience has made it necessary.

Still, the church has a mission to embrace. God has given the church the mission of being the place of discipleship. Not a discipleship that is primarily about learning, but one which is primarily concerned with the difficult process of growing. The truth is that all growth is painful, and the church has too often substituted education for transformation because the latter is too painful. The end result is that "normal Christians" are given the impression that spiritual growth and life transformation is supposed to come naturally and easily to those who are sincere and truly believe. Please, don't ever believe that or lead others to believe it.

The curriculum entitled Stickman Theology is meant to be a prerequisite to this course so that you can address any emotional, relational, or spiritual issues that may inhibit your application of this material to you life. This curriculum assumes you have studied Stickman Theology and are eager to continue your lifelong process of struggling, striving, and growing. So, grow on!

Chapter One

All Things are Permissible, but Not All are Beneficial

"Everything is permissible for me—but not everything is beneficial. Everything is permissible for me—but I will not be mastered by anything."

1 CORINTHIANS 6:12

Before we launch into our study of sin motivations, we want to make clear what it is that we are referring to when we use the word "sin." We are not referring to those who break someone else's rules, doubt someone's favorite non-essential doctrine, or fail to meet someone's lifestyle expectations. In this chapter we may well step on your toes by disagreeing with some things you have thought of as sin. Some behaviors, beliefs, and lifestyles you currently have categorized as right or wrong, good or bad, Christian or non-Christian may not be sinful at all. The first challenge this curriculum on sin motivations offers you is to examine what you can remove from your definition of sin. We are all too good at adding to our definition of sin.

Maybe you have noticed how self-righteous even the most callous of sinners can be. As an action-adventure movie addict, I've seen the bad guy blame the good guy for the crime he is committing. "If you try to stop me, I'll kill this beautiful young woman hostage (the hostages are almost always beautiful young women), and her death will be on your head," says the bad guy. And he means it. But, we know that the bad guy is wrong. He really is a bad guy, except for the movies where the bad guy is the hero. Robin

Hood and Jesse James had good reasons for being bad, and that made them good, right?

Don't laugh; you and I tend to tell ourselves the same things. We honestly believe that we would be less sinful if those around us were less sinful. However, the only test case for such a theory was the way that people responded to Jesus. His holiness didn't seem to eliminate the sinful nature of his disciples, and it obviously inflamed the sinful nature of those who called for and carried out his public torture and murder. And, they felt justified in doing so. So, before we go any further, let's agree to two things:

1) Our definition of sin tends to be too broad when applied to others, and
2) Our sin is not caused by others.

Remember, Jesus said, "Why do you look at the speck of sawdust in your brother's eye and pay no attention to the plank in your own eye?" (Mt 7:3).

This first chapter will focus on challenging us to stop fretting over the speck of sawdust in someone else's eye, so that we will be free to concentrate on the plank in our own.

Morals and Ethics

"It is better not to eat meat or drink wine or to do anything else that will cause your brother to fall. So whatever you believe about these things keep between yourself and God. Blessed is the man who does not condemn himself by what he approves."

ROMANS 14:21–22

Do you social drink? Do you go to R-rated movies? Do you let your children watch *Harry Potter* and trade the cards? Do you smoke? Is it wrong to "date" instead of "court"? How tight, revealing, and suggestive does clothing have to be before it's immoral to wear? Is body-piercing immoral? Can Christians listen to secular music?

These are just a few of the moral and ethical questions whose answers believers disagree on. Why? Is it because some Christians are just more committed than others, and if we were all committed to holiness, we would all agree as to what is and is not holy? I don't think so. Even though there are moral and ethical absolutes that God has given us (the Ten Commandments for instance), not every moral issue can be directly related to a scriptural mandate.

Paul faced this reality concerning whether it was permissible to eat meat sold in the market that came from animals that had been sacrificed in worship to idols. Paul addressed this moral issue as a relational issue (don't "do anything else that will cause your brother to fall" [Rom 14:21]). This was pretty wishy-washy moral direction. However, it was very clear and forceful relational advice.

It seems to me that the majority of our current moral issues fall into this same category. They should not be classified as moral issues but as relational issues. In so doing, we are really creating a mess for ourselves, but I believe it is an unavoidable mess. For instance; If my thirty-year-old son thinks that having tattoos will increase his effectiveness in reaching out to troubled youth, yet my parents think of having tattoos as a sign of rebellion and disrespect, how should I advise my son to resolve this "moral problem"? The answer is in not addressing this as a moral problem, but a relational one. I will advise my son to talk openly and honestly with his grandparents about what he is doing and why. If he values his relationship with his grandparents, and is convinced that God would have him be tattooed, he is obligated to explain to them his motives and thinking. They may or may not reach agreement, but respect and caring can still take place.

Of course all of this relational work could be avoided by simply labeling my son's desire to be tattooed as sin. Then he would be left with the simple choice of choosing what is right or what is wrong. No long discussions, sensitivity, respect, or honoring of each other would be needed. Do you really think that's what God desires for us?

Please consider this analogy: In scripture there are some moral absolutes. Let's refer to these absolutes as "red lights" (Stop! Don't do that!)

and "green lights" (Go! Do this!). If you do not honor the red and green lights, you are in rebellion to God. Repent, be forgiven, "go and sin no more." However, most of the moral directives of scripture are principles, not rules. Let's refer to these as "yellow lights" (Danger! Proceed with caution!). If my son were to claim that his decision to be tattooed was based upon a "green light" from God, I would question his maturity and preparedness to be in youth ministry. If his grandparents were to insist that being tattooed was violating a "red light" from God, I would question their sensitivity to and valuing of hurting people in our culture.

If we insist on making yellow light issues into red light or green light ones, we are forced to become legalistic snobs or disrespectful rebels. I believe it is more difficult to live with moral and ethical yellow lights than all red or green. With yellow lights, you have to be sensitive to God and others. You have to be willing to go forward with caution and be prepared to stop. You can't claim, "I have a right to...." You have to care for others more than you care for your alcohol (whether you drink it or not), your clothing, your earrings, your movies, etc. If you don't, your sin is not that you do any of these things or not, but that you don't love others as you should.

Those who have experienced the tragedy, misery, and waste created when people choose to violate the red lights in scripture may tend to want to put up speed blocks around the intersection, or set a police vehicle in plain view to deter any one who might run the red light. You can understand how these people could be motivated by love and get caught in the trap of legalism.

Those who have experienced the hypocrisy of legalistic Christians and been wounded by it may tend to try to protect others from the legalist by downplaying the danger broadcast by the yellow lights of scripture. They may argue that if the scripture doesn't prohibit something then there should be no reservations about it. You can understand how these people could be motivated by love and get caught in the trap of moral permissiveness.

Believe me, I would much rather have straight answers to the question, "Is this morally correct or not?" I want to know what is right, tell others what is right, and agree to hold each other accountable. But, that would be too easy. God looks at people's hearts. He sees their weaknesses, their igno-rance, their confusion, and their wounds. Then, he insists that those stronger in their faith make moral and ethical choices based upon the needs of the weaker. What a mess! Why doesn't he just allow the stronger ones to tell the weaker ones what is expected of them? (Isn't this our current "discipleship model"?) Isn't it much easier and more sensible for those stronger in their faith to simply teach the weak what they should and shouldn't do? Can't we avoid all this walking on eggshells? But, God didn't ask my advice. He tells me, "Whatever you believe about these things keep between yourself and God" (Rom 14:22).

Before we move on, let me give a concrete illustration of this prin-ciple. I'm thinking of the teenaged girl who realized that she did not experience the same kind of sexual attraction for boys that she did for other girls. She had heard teachings at church on the "sin of homosex-uality" and was afraid that she must be sinning. She had the courage to go to her youth director and tell him about her feelings. He referred her to their pastor, who referred her to me for counseling. Before we had her first session she was informed by her youth director that she could no longer serve in the leadership position she held in the youth group or continue to participate in the worship band. She came to our first ses-sion feeling very sad and very guilty.

During my ministry to this young lady I felt led to speak to the pastor and youth director to see if they would change their position toward my counselee. She had done absolutely nothing wrong. She had not nurtured or experimented with her same-sex attractions in any inappropriate ways. She had simply recognized and acknowledged her feelings. The pastor claimed to understand my position but felt bound to support the youth director in his "convictions." Thankfully, my counselee's parents were involved and supportive and chose to move their membership to another church. The parents recognized that their daughter's feelings were partially due to their own past difficulties; the father was celebrating two years of sobriety at the time.

The youth director had erred on the side of caution. He was willing to judge and reject the young lady based upon his fears of what she might say or do in the youth group. As understandable as the youth director's decision was, it was wrong! He took the easy way out. Instead of addressing the difficult yellow light issues related to the young lady's same-sex attractions, he declared her in violation of a red light. The message that my counselee received from her local church was that her feelings made her bad.

I offer this particular illustration because I believe the conservative churches in America are guilty of sending this same message to teenagers coming into awareness of their sexuality: "Sexual attractions are bad, especially same-sex attractions, and the stronger your feelings the worse you must be." The more difficult issues of embracing your sexual feelings and yet managing your sexual imaginations and behavior is lost behind the glare of the red lights flashing.

Theology and Doctrine

"Warn them before God against quarreling about words; it is of no value, and only ruins those who listen. Do your best to present yourself to God as one approved, a workman who does not need to be ashamed and who correctly handles the word of truth."

2 TIMOTHY 2:14–15

I believe that our issues of disagreement concerning theology and doctrine are of the same nature as our moral and ethical issues. There are essential doctrines of our faith that must not be compromised (green lights). There are non-essential doctrines of our faith that are beneficial to our growth and safeguard our heart and minds against heresy (yellow lights). And, there are heresies taught in the name of Christianity that betray the historical and literal truths of our faith (red lights).

Obviously, we have allowed the non-essentials of our faith to separate us, as evidenced by the number of denominations among us. Non-essential issues of our faith such as once-saved-always-saved as opposed to the its-possible-to-fall-from-grace doctrines are yellow light issues that sincere Bible-believing Christians have disagreed about for hundreds of years. When we try to solve this impasse by convincing each other of their theological error, we miss the point. But, if we let the issue become a relational one, there is a possibility of profound ministry taking place. For instance, If we know a member of our fellowship is practicing an ungodly lifestyle without repentance, it doesn't necessarily help to know if they were never really saved, or if they have fallen from grace, or if God is about to take them home ("the sin unto death"). We can leave those judgments to God as we go about our obligation to lovingly confront them and seeking to lead them to repentance, forgiveness, recommitment, and reconciliation.

The judgments that putting our theology first can force us into may actually get in the way of the ministry God has called us to. If we try to make these non-essential doctrines essential to someone's repentance and restoration to God, we are placing unnecessary obstacles in their path. On the other hand, if you decide to avoid the non-essentials of the faith you won't be able to minister to all the needs of a believer; in this case, an individual's need for assurance of their salvation. This is a yellow light issue.

The same is true for so many issues of our faith. Speaking in tongues, means of baptism, structure of the church leadership, etc. These are issues relevant to struggling, striving, and growing believers. However, the goal of any tenet of our faith is not to gain intellectual agreement, but to meet spiritual, emotional, or relational needs. We have to be able to get close enough to each other relationally to minister the helpful yellow light doctrines.

This does not mean that we can "spiritualize" the essential doctrine of our faith. That Jesus rose from the dead is a literal, historical fact. It is not a myth illustrating the truth that hope springs eternal. It is the basis in reality that makes the statement "hope springs eternal" true, rather than just an inspiring thought. If you are a part of a fellowship where the essential doctrines of our faith (a good synopsis is *The Apostle's Creed*) are not promoted as literal and historic realities, run away quickly (unless God has placed you there as a witness to others of the fellowship). If you are a part of a fellowship that insists on total agreement on the non-essential doctrines of our faith, run away quickly (same exemption applies).

In the World, But Not Of It

"For the pagans run after all these things, and your heavenly Father knows that you need them. But seek first his kingdom and his righteousness, and all these things will be given to you as well."

MATTHEW 6:32–33

"When you ask, you do not receive, because you ask with wrong motives, that you may spend what you get on your pleasures. You adulterous people, don't you know that friendship with the world is hatred toward God?"

JAMES 4:3–4a

In order to live in this world it takes money. Money, money, and more money. That's the way it is. It takes money to live in a house, drive a car, wear appropriate clothes, eat healthy (or unhealthy) meals, pay insurance, have a lawn mower, etc.—more if you're married, even more if you have children, more still if there are any health problems. We live in the world. But, we don't have to become captured by it. We don't have to invest our self-esteem, our hopes, our passions, or our joy in having expendable cash.

Again, we have to look for balance. Are there material things no Christian needs and cannot serve any godly function (red lights)? Yes. Are there material things that every Christian needs and can trust God to provide (green lights)? Yes. But, the green and red lights are few. The vast majority of material possessions could be used in a positive manner to serve God's purposes or could be used in a negative manner to distract from, inhibit, or substitute for God's purposes (yellow lights). The same relational dynamics should apply to this area of our lives as to the moral issues and theological issues. We must avoid blanket judgments, but be at ease raising the yellow light issues.

Is money a spiritually neutral substance, good or bad depending on how you use it? No! Money has a spiritual power within it to corrupt those who seek it, have it, or need more of it. It should not be a forbidden issue among those you fellowship with. Jesus spoke more about money than any other subject. Yet, among American Christians, the unwritten rule persists: "don't stick your nose in my business." This is an unbiblical relationship rule. If there is a reason why you need to drive an expensive car, why can't we talk about it? If you need a house that cost $X more than mine, tell me about it. If I seem to be irresponsible with my money, I need you to raise the issue with me. Money (or the lack thereof) does not define us as Christians in any way. We are in the world, but not of it. Our relationships need to be safe enough that money can be discussed.

Soon we will begin our study of sin motivations. In order to do so, in a healthy fashion, we must have some freedom to get past any legalism or license, any theological dogmatism or liberalism, and any defensiveness concerning our financial statuses and management. If you can't do so, you will not be able to go a step deeper in evaluating your sin motivations. God loves you passionately and is striving with you to gain your freedom from sin. Don't let any moral quibbles (like the way I use blunt illustrations), or non-essential doctrine (because this course is developed to avoid denominationally divisive issues), or lifestyle inhibitions (having too much, or having too little) distract you from a thorough self-examination. Those in your small group may question you concerning these things. We expect that you will try to answer honestly and fully.

If you have already come this far, you have demonstrated the courage and commitment to face these issues. We know it is not easy. It's not supposed to be. It is very understandable if you get upset or defensive, as long as you hang on and work through it! Growth is never easy. That's why we need each other. Press on. Others are counting on you.

Small Group Discussion

"As one who is in the Lord Jesus, I am fully convinced that no food is unclean in itself. But if anyone regards something as unclean, then for him it is unclean. If your brother is distressed because of what you eat, you are no longer acting in love. Do not by your eating destroy your brother for whom Christ died."

ROMANS 14:14–15

"So whatever you believe about these things keep between yourself and God. Blessed is the man who does not condemn himself by what he approves. But the man who has doubts is condemned if he eats, because his eating is not from faith; and everything that does not come from faith is sin."

ROMANS 14:22–23

Why does it have to be so complicated? Why doesn't God just say, "Yes, you can!" or "No, you can't!"? Discuss the following subjects as they relate to being red light or yellow light issues, and identify the point at which you believe these issues would be sin for you:

Communion wine	Soap operas
Nyquil	Marilyn Monroe standing on the air vent
Toasting the newlyweds	BayWatch
A beer after mowing the lawn	National Geographic
Wine with dinner	Artwork of pudgy nude women
A beer or two with friends	Artwork of provocatively posed pudgy
A beer or two before bed	nude women (with no arms)
A four-beer birthday bash	Lingering over a magazine or internet site
"When I need to relax" six-pack	found by accident
A "let's forget it" case of beer	Playful suggestive chatting on the internet
Etc., etc.... Alcoholism	Etc., etc.... Sexual addiction

All Things are Permissible, but Not All are Beneficial

Divide into groups of two or three and discuss the following three statements:

1) Yellow lights are about personal introspection and integrity. Each person should diligently examine their thoughts and feelings to discern when and how they are being negatively affected by elements of this world.

"Everything is permissible—but not everything is beneficial. Everything is permissible—but not everything is constructive."

1 CORINTHIANS 10:23

2) Yellow lights are about reaching the "unchurched," not conforming to the comfort level of those in the church. The church is not the guardian of our cultures' traditions, but a safe place for God to touch and heal our hearts, minds, and souls.

"When Peter came to Antioch, I opposed him to his face, because he was clearly in the wrong. Before certain men came from James, he used to eat with the Gentiles. But when they arrived, he began to draw back and separate himself from the Gentiles because he was afraid of those who belonged to the circumcision group. The other Jews joined him in his hypocrisy, so that by their hypocrisy even Barnabas was led astray."

GALATIANS 2:11–13

3) Get together in your small groups and pray for one another.

Chapter Two

If I Knew, I Wouldn't Need You to Tell Me

In this chapter we will look at the difficult tasks of self-reflection and self-acceptance.

Self-reflection is the ability to see yourself the way that God or others see you. Self-acceptance is the ability to embrace what has been made known to you through self-reflection.

My wife and I were arguing about who said what. I remembered her having repeated the same negative comment (about something I felt positively about: me) at least three times during our supper with two other couples. After telling how we remembered it several times through, I came up with the logical solution: we should call one of the other couples and ask them how they remembered it. My wife was so sure that she was right that she agreed, despite her embarrassment in revealing to our friends that we were arguing. This was an important moment for us, because my wife too often remembered things in ways that I thought put me in a negative light. More than just this one argument was riding on this phone call.

I was unfortunate enough to reach the wife of the couple I called for confirmation. Being a woman, naturally, she remembered the conversation the same way my wife did. So, nothing was resolved for us that night. Just kidding. Actually, our friend did remember the conversation the way my wife did, and I repeated this test after two more disagreements between Shaun and I that followed. On each occasion the objective third party agreed with Shaun. With my finely honed skills of self-reflection (ha!), I was able to reach a conclusion about myself after only twenty-three years of such arguments. I finally realized that I tend to remember things the way that suits me best.

I can honestly say that I do not intentionally misrepresent how things happened and who said what. I truly remember those situations just like I said I did, I just remembered them wrong. However, there is a truth about myself that I was forced to recognize many years ago; I am a prideful person. Pride is one of two Seven Deadly Sins that I struggle with the most. So, I believe that my remembering inaccurately is due to my pride. My pride is so inherent to me that I don't always recognize when I'm acting it out.

So, now that I've exercised self-reflection (aided by my wife), I have the option of exercising self-acceptance or not. I can openly acknowledge my struggle with pride and ask my wife (and others) to help me recognize my sin, or I can feel ashamed of myself and promise myself (and others) that I will never act like that again (denial).

Self-acceptance does not mean giving into my sin and insisting that others "accept me as I am." It means that I remain aware of my tendencies and take responsibility for any offense I may create. It means that I still value myself as a struggling, striving, and growing Christian. My sin does not change the good aspects of my relationship with God or others unless I refuse to honestly acknowledge and take responsibility for the hurtful things I do. Self-acceptance does not mean that I can only think good thoughts about myself. It means that I embrace the positives along with the negatives and believe that God continues to love me and use me. It is only when I refuse to accept myself that I begin to feel defensive toward others and rejected by God.

Crisis Revelations

If I do not intentionally practice self-reflection, I will not be aware of my sin motivations until I create a crisis for myself.

One such crisis came early in my pastoral ministry. I was pastor of a small congregation while studying for my undergraduate degree in psychology. This small church embraced me as their pastor, although I was only twenty years old and unqualified. They provided a salary and a parsonage for my pregnant wife, my son, and myself. They were humble people who considered it their ministry "to help young preachers get started." I appreciated their acceptance and didn't mind being called "lad," but I had other expectations that they were not meeting. One of my expectations for them was voted down in a board meeting that took place during our regular Sunday school time. I was surprised and upset. I didn't know what to say. It was time for our worship service to begin, and we proceeded as normal. Throughout the service, and even as I preached, I was nursing my anger and thinking of what I wished I had said in the board meeting. As I concluded the service, I asked the congregation to return to their seats for a moment so I could make an announcement. Then, I launched into a fifteen-minute lecture/scolding of the entire congregation.

When I finally ran out of words, a dear woman stood and began speaking calmly. She first expressed, on behalf of the congregation, her respect and admiration for me. Then she gently pointed out that my lecture was inappropriate and was part of a larger pattern I had, which, she concluded, was that I spoke to them as if they were spiritual babies.

Anyone else would have been relieved at the gentleness of her rebuke, and the opportunity to address the bigger issue. Not me. I did see them as spiritual babies (otherwise, why would they accept a twenty-year-old pastor?), but I wasn't ready to admit that to myself, and certainly not to them. So, instead of making an appropriate response, I reacted. To her conclusions that I spoke to them as if they were spiritual babies I replied, "Well, consider it a compliment, because I don't even know if that much is true," and I stormed out of the church.

In other words, I created a crisis for myself. My pride and anger had been exposed for the world to see. Still, believe it or not, I seriously considered adopting the belief that what I had done was justified and that God was speaking through me prophetically to the congregation. To this day, I could still make a case for that perspective. (If you would like to hear it, I would enjoy explaining it to you.) However, God made the truth known to me, and I spent most of the next week asking forgiveness of each individual that had been present.

Is Self-Reflection a Lost Art?

The previous story is just one illustration of what I call "crisis revelations." I could give any number of personal illustrations. I could give thousands of illustrations from those I have counseled. Sometimes, I feel like maybe the Body of Christ has lost all ability at self-reflection and can only truly see their sin motivations through crisis revelations. Although Jesus told us that "anyone who is [continually] angry with his brother will be subject to judgment" (Mt 5:22a), and that "anyone who looks at a woman lustfully has already committed adultery with her in his heart" (Mt 5:28), we seldom take the necessary steps to face our sin motivations until we have actually been caught in the act.

Some may say, "Terry, your perspective on the church has been tainted by your counseling practice. Of course you see those who are not good at self-reflection. That's why they are in counseling." But, I disagree. I have met very few people, in my counseling practice or otherwise, who seem capable of honest self-reflection.

Recently, I agreed to present a seminar for the small group leaders of a church in a nearby city. Twenty-eight leaders or co-leaders were present. At the first session, I felt impressed to ask them about their personal accountability practice. I described the nature of intimate accountability and gave a couple of personal illustrations. I then asked for a show of hands of those who were currently participating in intimate accountability. Not one hand went up. I was a little surprised, so I ask a broader question. How many had ever experienced intimate accountability? This time, two hands were raised.

And you may say, "Hold on, Terry. You just changed the issue. You were talking about our ability to practice self-reflection, then you changed over to whether or not we participated in intimate accountability." However, I don't think it is a change of issues. I don't think we can practice honest self-reflection without intimate accountability. Or, if you can, you are a better person than I am. I have a tendency to think that the way I think is a perfectly fine way to think. If I didn't, I probably wouldn't have thought that way in the first place. Hence, the title to this chapter: If I knew, I wouldn't need you to tell me.

I need those around me who love me enough to help me see myself through their eyes. Left to myself, I will not be able to gain freedom from my own perspectives. Even when confronted by scripture or books on discipleship, I'm capable of agreeing with what I read, but not applying it to a situation I'm involved in the next day. Why? Because I am motivated to forget, misinterpret, or misapply what I've learned. And so are you. Your motivation may be different from mine, but we all have sin motivations that work subtly on our thinking, attitudes, and behaviors. The art of self-reflection is found in our ability to identify those motivations. Therefore, we are offering the Seven Deadly Sins as a tool for identifying your sin motivations and enabling your practice of self-reflection.

Maybe you are taking this course because you created a crisis for yourself and someone has insisted that you "get some help for yourself." Or maybe taking this course is part of your ongoing commitment to self-reflection. Either way, we thank you for joining us in assuring that the Body of Christ will not lose the art of self-reflection.

Is Self-Acceptance a Lost Virtue?

Do you consider self-acceptance (as defined earlier in this chapter) to be a virtue? Jesus did. I know because in the fourth chapter of Matthew I can read about the temptations that Jesus faced, and, I can tell you, they are not exactly like any that I have ever faced. These temptations were unique to Jesus (although the sin motivations behind them were not). There is only one way we could know about Jesus' personal temptations. He must have told his disciples about them. And, since I can't imagine that Jesus was ashamed of his temptation (and neither should we be), he was being accepting of himself. He accepted the fact that the ideas Satan presented were appealing to him. He was tempted. Strongly tempted. Satan knew how to push Jesus' buttons. Matthew 4 is not a record of Jesus' contest of intelligence with Satan, or a battle of wills; it was Satan offering things to Jesus that his flesh hungered after.

Do you think that Jesus felt the same aching pain of longing for some "forbidden fruit" that you and I have felt? Do you think he ever felt the pent-up energy of anger, lust, or pride pressing for release? Do you think he ever felt the awful weight of sloth, envy, or gluttony pressing upon him to stop caring or to just do nothing? Scripture says that he did: "Because he himself suffered when he was tempted, he is able to help those who are being tempted" (Heb 2:18). Jesus accepted the fact that he was more subject to some temptations than others. That is the very heart of self-acceptance.

You and I need to exercise this virtue. Without it, we may be able to practice self-reflection and understand our motivations after we have sinned, but we will not be prepared for encountering our next temptation. Without the virtue of self-acceptance, every time we are tempted is like the first time. We are unaware, unprepared, and will probably not be able to resist. By accepting the nature of our sin motivations, we will not be surprised by the unique suffering our temptations bring us. We will become more aware of what circumstances create high-temptation situations for us, and how to avoid them. We will be able to face the suffering caused by our temptations without shame. We will be much more likely to call on Jesus in the midst of our temptation, because we will understand that he knows how we actually feel. Our acceptance of our unique sin motivations is a virtue.

The alternatives to the virtue of self-acceptance are too numerous to name, but a small listing of types of self-rejection might be helpful:

- Denial—refusing to acknowledge that you have any unique sin motivations.
- Guilt—anger at yourself for the fact that you can be tempted at all.
- Searing of Conscience—deciding that since the suffering of the temptation cannot be avoided that it is somehow okay to act out, in sin, to relieve the suffering.
- Sense of Victimization—thinking that no one else suffers with temptations the way you do.
- Religious Zeal—directing the majority of your efforts toward holiness into correcting/avoiding the "worldly" sources of your temptation.
- Doctrinal Zeal—defending certain non-essential doctrine in

hopes of safeguarding your relationship with God despite your sins (for instance; speaking in tongues as evidence of being filled with the Holy Spirit may be a biblically held belief or a way of assuring yourself of your own spirituality).

- Legalism—deciding that some sins (usually not your own) are greater evidence of hardness of heart toward God than others.
- Privacy—maintaining that the more personal aspects of your thinking and feeling should remain private to the extent that no one really gets to know you.

The list could go on and on.

The alternatives to self-acceptance are subtle and progressive. Once we find a coping mechanism (other than self-acceptance) that helps us feel better about our sin motivations, we will come to rely upon it more and more. The coping mechanism becomes a stronghold in our life that may never let us go.

In *The Great Divide,* C. S. Lewis gives a mythical account of a man with a demon attached to his back, who is standing on the outskirts of heaven. The man cannot progress further into heaven unless he denounces his demon. It is a painful struggle for him, but once the demon is rejected, it immediately is transformed into a white stallion that carries the man into the depths of heaven. I believe our coping mechanisms are like that demon. When they are rejected, they are transformed into self-acceptance, the white stallion that will carry us into the depth of the kingdom of God!

> *"Therefore, since we have a great high priest who has gone through the heavens, Jesus the Son of God, let us hold firmly to the faith we profess. For we do not have a high priest who is unable to sympathize with our weaknesses, but we have one who has been tempted in every way, just as we are—yet was without sin. Let us then approach the throne of grace with confidence, so that we may receive mercy and find grace to help us in our time of need."*

HEBREWS 4:14–16

Small Group Discussion

1) Give an account of a time you created a crisis for yourself, and state what the crisis revealed about you.

2) Name one thing you learned in this chapter that you believe will be of help to you.

3) Pray for one another.

Chapter Three

Sin Motivations and Sin Manifestations

L et's examine one more principle before we begin studying each of the Seven Deadly Sins individually.

In this chapter we want to clarify the difference between our sin motivations and our sin manifestations and discuss how they relate to each other. So, let's begin with our definitions.

SIN MOTIVATIONS: The scheme proposed by Satan to meet our legitimate needs in inappropriate ways. (We will identify these schemes in the broad categories of the Seven Deadly Sins.)

SIN MANIFESTATIONS: The physical acting out of our sin motivations.

Based upon these definitions, we will offer three principles for your consideration:

1) Any sin motivation can lead to any sin manifestation.
2) Lack of obvious sin manifestations does not indicate a lack of sin motivations.
3) The more compelling our sin motivations become, the less able we are to identify and/or address them appropriately.

Joe (not his real name) came in for counseling after his wife had caught him downloading pornography off the internet. He knew he had a problem, but had not acknowledged his inability to resist the temptation (self-reflection), let alone admit his need for help (self-acceptance). In short, he had created a crisis for himself. Now, his wife was upset, she had insisted he talk to his pastor, and his pastor had sent him for counseling.

When he met with me, he told me that he knew what he was doing was wrong and he was not going to do it anymore. I asked him if he knew why he was doing it. He claimed he just happened upon it and then made a habit of returning to it. I asked him if he knew why he kept returning to it. He said it was just the natural thing for a man to do. I pressed a little, saying, "Oh, so your dad does it, and soon your son will be doing it also?"

"No, and *no!*" Joe replied. "That's not what I said."

"Yes, it is what you said, but now, tell me what you meant," I prodded him.

"I meant that it just seemed like the natural thing to do. But, I know it was wrong, and I'm not going to do it again."

"So, before your wife caught you, you didn't know what you were doing was wrong. But now that she is all upset, and you visited with your pastor, you have figured out that what you were doing was wrong?"

"No," Joe leaned back on the couch and sighed. "I knew it was wrong all along."

"Then, let me ask you again, Joe, why did you do it?"

Slowly Joe lifted his eyes from the carpet and looked into mine. Meekly he claimed, "I don't know."

I gave him an encouraging smile and said, "Well, then, you are in the right place. I can help you with that if you want me to."

"Yeah, I really do," he replied. And, we began to work on finding out why Joe had been viewing pornography.

You may be thinking, "I know why Joe was looking at pornography. It was lust, pure and simple." And, in some cases you might be right (although, not in Joe's case). But, let's say you were right. Joe was motivated by lust. Then what?

1) Joe would need to acknowledge the nature of lust (denying or exaggerating someone or something's spiritual significance) and repent (turn away) from it by learning how to challenge himself to assign appropriate spiritual significance to himself,

other people, and things. This would be one way to address the spiritual root of his lust.

2) Joe would need to understand why stripping or exaggerating others' spiritual significance was appealing to him. What was the draw? Why did pornography make him feel better? What emotional need was it serving? This would be one way to address the emotional root of his lust.

3) Joe would need to learn how to represent his appropriate sexual motivations in his relationship with his wife (which she might or might not be open to). This would be one way to address the relational root of his lust.

Joe would need to develop self-reflection and self-acceptance as a sexual being. It would be a spiritually, emotionally, and relationally difficult process. However, this particular "Joe" was not motivated by lust. We discovered that his sin motivations were anger and sloth. The sin manifestation was lust. His sin motivations could just as easily have been manifested in theft, verbal abuse, plotting revenge, or directed toward himself and turned into symptoms of crippling arthritis or a weighty depression.

Without self-reflection, Joe would have been unable to identify his sin motivations. ("After all, it was a sexual sin, so why not call it lust?" claim those who have lost the art of self-reflection.) And, without self-acceptance, Joe would have been unable to address the emotional and relational issues fueling his sin motivations. (Those who no longer value self-acceptance may say, "Give him a break, it wasn't that big a deal," or "We all have to control ourselves, so tell him to ignore his feelings and do what is right.")

Any motivational sin can create any manifestation of sin. The early Christian Church fathers identified the Seven Deadly Sins of sloth, pride, anger, greed, gluttony, lust, and envy as "motivational sins." If you were an irresponsible person, our first guess would be that your sin motivation is sloth. However, let's assume your irresponsibility is really motivated by anger. Your irresponsibility is a passive way of punishing others, or passively protecting yourself from expectations that you think are inappropriate.

Let's pretend that your irresponsibility began when you passively rebelled from your parents' expectations (appropriate or not). Furthering the imagined scenario, we hear your parents confronting your irresponsible behavior and telling you that you are lazy and slothful. So, now your parents have discerned (incorrectly) your motivations for you. But, you are just a child. It makes sense to assume that your parents are right. You cry and tell your parents you are sorry for being lazy. Life goes on, and you grow up.

While growing up, you find yourself being irresponsible from time to time. Sometimes it is because you are motivated by anger, sometimes by gluttony, other times (your parents are right) you are honestly slothful, and at other times you are legitimately tired or forgot to do something. But every time, you (or your parents), call yourself slothful. Your predominant sin manifestation is sloth, but your sin motivation is primarily anger.

You get married. For some reason, you marry a person with high expectations of you. You have always resented high expectations, but you really do love your wife and want to please her. Sometimes you do, sometimes you don't. It seems to you that you get little praise from your wife for the times you meet her expectations. And, it seems to you that the times you fail are remembered forever. This feeds your anger, but you don't acknowledge it. Instead, you feel the stronger grip of your sin manifestation. For some reason, you just don't get around to the things that others are trusting you for.

Your wife gets upset and lists all the times you've failed to follow through. You sincerely repent of your slothfulness, and commit yourself to doing better. And, you try. For some reason, it is harder than it should be. Sometimes you succeed, sometimes you fail. Your wife voices the complaint again. Again, you repent and promise to do better. But, now, your wife doesn't trust you. She decides that you really don't love her and suggests you talk with your pastor.

You and your wife go to your pastor and explain the situation. The pastor assists you in drawing up a list of agreements as to what you will be responsible for. Trying to prove your love to your wife, you agree to even more responsibilities than before. Your true sin motivation (anger) begins to interpret the whole scenario as emotional blackmail by your wife and legalism by your pastor. You are way past the point of acknowledging those thoughts (you feel them more than think them), but they still impact you.

To make a long story short, you fail in keeping your agreements. Now, you are embarrassed to talk with your pastor, so you are avoiding church (another manifestation of sloth?). Your wife has learned not to trust you, and begins to question whether or not you are even saved. You have honestly tried, sincerely repented when you failed, and are beginning to doubt God. You think, "Maybe my wife is right. I think I'll ask the pastor about being re-baptized." And on it goes. Again and again, you repent of your sloth, and you sincerely, wholeheartedly ask God to deliver you from sloth. But your irresponsibility remains in place because you've misidentified your motivation and you haven't allowed God to minister to your anger.

Lack of obvious sin manifestations does not indicate a lack of sin motivations. Sometimes our sin manifestations are very subtle and can even be represented as virtues. For instance, the businessman can represent pride as integrity or diligence or even love for his family. His pride may be the motivation for making his business a success, but he may never acknowledge it. And, although his wife and children will probably recognize it for what it is, the rest of the world may praise him for it.

One of the most devastating schemes of Satan involves pride among pastors. I have presented the analogy of the stickman and the strongman as representatives of spiritual maturity to dozens of pastors. Never has a single pastor questioned the biblical accuracy of identifying the stickman clinging to the armor of God as an analogy of spiritual maturity. Never has a single pastor questioned my claim that the spiritual strongman is a myth and a fraudulent analogy of spiritual maturity. Yet, all too often, the pastors report that their congregation expects them to act like the spiritual strongman. These pastors don't believe they can be transparent in the pulpit.

Satan tells them that they are representing God, not themselves. The lie is wrapped in many different packages, but the message to the pastor is the same: "Don't let your congregation know that you are a struggling, striving, and growing Christian. What hope will they have if they can't see a 'successful' Christian leader? You need to be the living, breathing proof that 'Jesus purifies us from sin.' And, if you have to give an example of your own sin, tell about something that happened years ago and how you have been set free of it."

Recently, a pastor told me that if the leaders of his church knew that he and his teenage son were having such problems they might ask him to resign. He did not want members of his church to know that he was seeking help. He was convinced that his church members would be disappointed in him and maybe even their faith in God would be shaken if they knew their pastor needed help relating to his son. The temptation to pride, disguised as leadership or encouragement or even faith is constantly before our pastors. It seems to me to be one of Satan's most commonly applied and successful schemes.

These are just a couple of examples of the fact that our sin motivations aren't always manifested in obvious ways. I wish my sins were more obvious, not to everyone else, but at least to me. If there were a Jiminy Cricket riding on my shoulder, who would tell me every time I was acting on my sin motivations even when I looked good doing it, it would be helpful to me.

You may say, "There is a Jiminy Cricket on your shoulder; it's called 'your conscience.'"

Yes, but my conscience can be mistrained, seared, or even too sensitive. My conscience (guilt feelings) can tell me I've sinned when I really haven't and can tell me I haven't when I really have. Our conscience has to be properly trained! That is one of the goals of our spiritual disciplines. Since our parents were dysfunctional in some ways (and if you haven't figured out in what ways your parents were dysfunctional, then you have not progressed very far in the art of self-reflection), they contributed to mistraining your conscience. Our culture, fallen as it is, has also contributed to mistraining your conscience. Your friends, sinful as they are, have made their contributions. Even your church has probably contributed. This process of self-reflection is not just a matter of "following your conscience." It will not come naturally or easily.

The more compelling our sin motivations become, the less able we are to identify and/or address them appropriately. It is often true that the greater our sin motivations become (reaching the status of strongholds), the more skilled we become in hiding our motivations, finding others who accommodate our sin manifestations, or representing our sins as virtues. In *People of the Lie,* M. Scott Peck presents these dynamics in shockingly revealing detail. "The lie" that he refers to is that some people have a great motivation to look good, but no motivation to be good. Their lives become a lie. And, although they are highly emotionally, relationally, and spiritually damaged people, they may function very well socially. These people rarely end up in therapy. Their family members become the "identified problem."

It's true: some of our strongholds are less obvious than others'. Some have consequences that are more immediately painful (allowing us to create a crisis for ourselves). But, some of our sin motivations will never be revealed by sin manifestations. We can all live the lie to one extent or another. So, ultimately, you have to desire to know God and His righteousness (not just avoid sin) in order to develop the art of self-reflection.

By the time our sin motivations have become compulsions, they have sunk roots into our souls. They have become strongholds within us. These strongholds have three roots driven into our souls to support themselves: a spiritual root, an emotional root, and a relational root (see *Stickman Theology*). These strongholds cannot be removed from our lives without addressing all three roots. It will not be enough to get right with God unless you also get right with yourself (emotionally) and get right with others (relationally). Removing any one or two roots of the sin motivation will not serve to pull down the stronghold.

My understanding is that there are some churches out there that do a wonderful job ministering to the spiritual needs of people by clarifying the nature of God and calling upon us to embrace truth. They are addressing the spiritual roots. Therefore, people will repent, they'll make new commitments, they'll practice spiritual disciplines, and they will deal with that spiritual root. Then, the expectation is that the stronghold will go away. But, once it has been established, a stronghold cannot be pulled up by just one or two roots. We have to deal with all three roots, emotional, relational, and spiritual. Our study of the Seven Deadly Sins will take each of these into account.

So, let me conclude with these thoughts. All Christians have strongholds in their lives. You've never met one who doesn't, you've never heard them on the radio, and you've never seen them on television. There is no such thing as a Christian without strongholds. Therefore, this is our declaration today: Those who acknowledge their strongholds and embrace the spiritual warfare in order to pull them down are the bold and courageous among the Body of Christ.

Small Group Discussion

1) Share whether the information in this chapter tended to make you feel discouraged or encouraged, and why.

2) Talk about whether or not you feel prepared to study the Seven Deadly Sins without inappropriate guilt and shame.

3) Pray for one another.

Chapter Four

Pride

"For a man's ways are in full view of the Lord, and he examines all his paths. The evil deeds of a wicked man ensnare him; the cords of his sin hold him fast."

PROVERBS 5:21–22

Pride is disagreeing with God concerning our character and/or our attributes.

When we disagree with God concerning our attributes, we are judging God. If I think that my attributes (physical traits, talents, personality, etc.) somehow thwart God's ability to provide a wonderful and valuable life for me, I have a pride problem. Some think this is low self-esteem. It is not. Low self-esteem is when we recognize our strengths, but they have been devalued and rejected by people who are important to us so that the best we have to offer has been stripped of its significance. But, when I tell myself that God really didn't do right by me, I am judging God. If I think I should be taller, I should be able to sing better, I should be more intelligent, I should be more athletic, I should be more capable in math, then I am disparaging the attributes of who I am, and I have a pride problem.

"For in his own eyes he flatters himself too much to detect or hate his sin."

PSALM 36:2

Disagreeing with God concerning our character is arrogance. If I don't acknowledge my sin motivations, or consider them less significant than the sin motivations of others, I have a pride problem. In this chapter and the following six, I challenge you to work hard at identifying and analyzing your basic sin motivations. Do not reject the opportunity to repent. Do not reject the conviction of the Holy Spirit when it comes. This course is one of the opportunities God has created to lead you to repentance by His kindness. If you harden your heart to His kindness, His love for you will require Him to try to break your hardened heart.

Jesus' Words to the Proud

In the verses that follow I want to make one slight modification to the NIV translation. Where the NIV has translated Jesus' words as "Woe to you," I have changed them to "Damn you." This modification is not for dramatic effect but represents what I believe to be an accurate interpretation. I'm asking you to read the following verses aloud. Please try to let your tone and volume match the nature of Jesus' words even if you have to read it aloud several times.

> [Damn you], teachers of the law and Pharisees, you hypocrites! You shut the kingdom of heaven in men's faces. You yourselves do not enter, nor will you let those enter who are trying to. [Damn you], teachers of the law and Pharisees, you hypocrites! You devour the widows' houses and for a show make lengthy prayers. Therefore you will be punished more severely. [Damn you], teachers of the law and Pharisees, you hypocrites! You travel over land and sea to win a single convert, and when he becomes one, you make him twice as much a son of hell as you are. [Damn you], blind guides! You say, "If anyone swears by the temple, it means nothing; but if anyone swears by the gold of the temple, he is bound by his oath." You blind fools! Which is greater: the gold, or the temple that makes the gold sacred? You also say, "If anyone swears by the altar, it means nothing; but if anyone swears by the gift on it, he is bound by his oath." You blind men! Which is greater: the gift, or the altar that makes the gift sacred? Therefore, he who swears by the altar swears by it

and by everything on it. And he who swears by the temple swears by it and the by one who dwells in it. And he who swears by heaven swears by God's throne and by the one who sits on it. [Damn you], teachers of the law and Pharisees, you hypocrites! You give a tenth of your spices—mint, dill and cummin. But you have neglected the more important matters of the law—justice, mercy and faithfulness. You should have practiced the latter, without neglecting the former. You blind guides! You strain out a gnat but swallow a camel. [Damn you], teachers of the law and Pharisees, you hypocrites! You clean the outside of the cup and dish, but inside they are full of greed and self-indulgence. Blind Pharisee! First clean the inside of the cup and dish, and then the outside also will be clean. [Damn you], teachers of the law and Pharisees, you hypocrites! You are like whitewashed tombs, which look beautiful on the outside but on the inside are full of dead men's bones and everything unclean. In the same way, on the outside you appear to people as righteous but on the inside you are full of hypocrisy and wickedness. [Damn you], teachers of the law and Pharisees, you hypocrites! You build tombs for the prophets and decorate the graves of the righteous. And you say, "If we had lived in the days of our forefathers, we would not have taken part with them in shedding the blood of the prophets." So you testify against yourselves that you are the descendants of those who murdered the prophets. Fill up, then, the measure of the sin of your forefathers!

MATTHEW 23:13–32

Commentaries make it clear that the title "Pharisee" can be characterized by two traits: legalism and pride. Jesus is trying to break through that legalism and confront the pride. He is calling for repentance. He is calling for humbling. In the process, he defines the seven manifestations of pride. I want to walk through them with you.

Terry Ewing

Seven Manifestations of Pride

1) REJECTING GRACE-BASED RELATIONSHIPS

First, in verse 13, Jesus claims that pride shuts the kingdom of heaven in men's faces. What is the kingdom of heaven all about? The law had been given to establish a "punishment due" for our sins. Now, with the coming of the kingdom of God, we are offered grace and mercy. So, the first manifestation of pride is to reject a relationship based on grace. If you gain nothing else from your study of this chapter, I hope you remember this point: Every healthy relationship we have is a relationship based upon grace.

Pride says just the opposite. Pride says, "I want you to love me, because I am so wonderful. I want to win your love and win your faithfulness and win your attention and win your approval, because that proves that I am a valuable." While Gods says, "You have nothing to prove. You are who you are, because I created you as you are."

In our culture there are too few examples of godly relationships, but I want to point out one format on television today that is a wonderful illustration of healthy relationships: the sitcom. I don't get the chance to watch sitcoms often, and usually there is enough bad incorporated in them that you may not want to watch them. But they are all based upon this one premise: All these people have a problem, and everybody knows they have a problem. We laugh at them, because they love each other and they are committed to each other even though they are each one a jerk in his own way. These are relationships based upon grace; otherwise Gilligan's Island would be a nightmare, and none of us could love Lucy. Regardless of how crazy and wacky and fundamentally dysfunctional they are, the other characters love and respect these sitcom characters. I want you to know that is a good model of relational health. And that is what we want to be able to receive for ourselves. We want to be able to say, "I am a sitcom character." And you are a sitcom character. We need relationships based on grace.

2) BEING SPIRITUAL BULLIES

Another manifestation of pride is when we take advantage of others' weaknesses.

In verse 14, Jesus claims that pride leads to spiritual bullying. The Pharisees promoted themselves as spiritual strongmen, whose prayers meant more to God than those of others, in order to give them control over others. Then, they used that control to manipulate and abuse those who trusted them the most.

They made a show of lengthy prayers while devouring widows' houses. Doesn't that sound just like the accusation we hear about television evangelists? And, on occasion, those accusations have been proven true. An example you may recall what took place in my hometown of Tulsa, Oklahoma, where reporters televised trash bins full of discarded prayer requests. The story was told of one of the TV preachers who asked his listeners to send in prayer requests along with their donations (to the "spiritual strongman" whose prayers were supposedly so powerful). The preacher had promised to pray over each request individually. But, news shows reported that his mail was being processed by a company that collected the contributions and threw the prayer requests away without anyone recording them or praying over them.

Jesus made it clear that the Pharisees were being bullies, based upon the presumed spiritual weakness of others. We can be spiritual bullies, beating others down with our superior knowledge of scripture. We can be physical bullies, pushing around the littler kids on the playground. We can be social bullies, excluding the less attractive or successful from our lives. It is all based upon pride.

3) DESIRING THE DEVOTION OF OTHERS
A third manifestation of pride is when we desire the devotion of others.

The Pharisees went to all lengths to draw people and convert them and it makes them "twice the son of hell" as they were. In other words, their motivation wasn't to convert people to Judaism for the sake of others' spiritual needs; they were converting people to be their pupils, to be their disciples, to be devoted to them. That is the nature of pride, and we all struggle with it. It begins very early in our lives, when we want to win each other's approval. Whether it is athletics or grades or dating or even our kids' successes and failures, we want others to think we are better than we are. Sometimes we want our kids to be good just because it makes us look good. Well, that's a very prideful thing.

Let me give this illustration, because I think it makes the case so very, very well. Which is healthier, which is more appropriate? Should my wife be faithful to me because I am such a wonderful person, so attractive to her that I hold her devotion and love and I am able to create this devotion that she has toward me? Or should she be faithful to me just because that is the way she is and what she promised to do? Pride says that she should be faithful to me because I'm so wonderful. Yet, that makes for a very insecure relationship, because I'm not always so very wonderful. From this insecurity grows the need for more pride (to calm the insecurity that pride created), and that is how we become ensnared by our sin.

God has offered us a relational alternative. He has called us to join together because we share a vision, we share a cause, we share a calling, and we share a commitment. Then, when our stickman aspects start coming out, we don't run each other off, because that is not why we were there in the first place. But the proud person seeks the devotion of others.

4) Setting Subjective Standards

A fourth manifestation of pride is when we set our own subjective standards.

The Pharisees claimed that swearing by the temple meant nothing, but if you were swearing by the gold of the temple the oath was binding. They were creating their own system of vows, subjectively deciding which ones were significant and which ones were not. We still play that game today, and I want to use an illustration that is very controversial. At what point have we broken our marriage vows (see Mt 19:7–9)? If you are thinking the answer is "when one of us commits adultery or when we legally divorce," I believe you are wrong. That is just the gold on the altar; that is not the altar itself. The marriage vows are to love, honor, and respect each other. We break our marriage vows when we stop loving, honoring, and respecting. If we are unrepentant in our unfaithfulness to our wedding vows, we may or may not manifest that unfaithfulness (hardness of heart) in adultery. Yet, unrepentant disrespect and dishonoring of a spouse will lead to rejection, isolation, bitterness, and "divorce" within one's heart. All too often, we deal with divorce like the Pharisees would; we define it by a legal process rather than by a relational reality.

The Pharisees put all the value on appearances. That is the nature of pride.

5) PROMOTING SELF-SERVING LEGALISTIC STANDARDS

Jesus presses on by identifying the Pharisees' practice of legalistically promoting their own subjective, self-serving standards.

Which standard did the Pharisees elevate above others? Tithing. Why do you think the Pharisees and the scribes chose to make such a big deal out of tithing? What was their motivation? Could it be because they were depending on that money? When others followed their example and gave their tithe, the Pharisees got the money. It went for their support. Of course they wanted everyone else to tithe. Jesus did not say they shouldn't have promoted tithing, but that there were weightier matters that were being neglected. Pride encourages promoting self-serving standards. Humility moves us to promote those standards that are most difficult for us.

6) BEING OVERLY CONCERNED FOR OUTWARD APPEARANCES

A sixth manifestation of pride is when we become overly concerned for outward appearances.

We are guilty of this manifestation of pride when we don't feel bad about ourselves when we sin, but we feel really bad when we get caught. For a proud person, sin is not sin until he gets caught—until there are consequences. Pride is not wounded by our moral failures, but when others come to know about our failures. If no one knows of his failure, the proud person feels no shame. Worse still, the proud person can get very angry when his sin is revealed. Instead of feeling guilt, he becomes bitter.

7) IMAGINING OURSELVES TO BE NOBLE

The seventh manifestation Jesus points out is that pride leads us to imagine ourselves to be noble in other circumstances.

The Pharisees claimed that had they been alive in the days of Isaiah,

Jeremiah, and Ezekiel, they surely would not have participated in persecuting them. Yet, here they were, persecuting Jesus. The Pharisees' pride had totally deluded them. They had a noble idea of themselves, even as they practiced sin.

Pride affects us in the same way. We tend to see ourselves as noble. For instance, had you lived as a plantation owner, in the South, prior to the Civil War, what would you have done in regard to slavery? Of course, we would all like to imagine that we would have been actively sacrificing ourselves to end that evil. Pride leads us to think of ourselves that way. But, what would you really have done?

I can tell you what you would have done, and you can tell me what I would have done. We would have done the same kinds of things that we have done concerning the abortion issue. Whatever you are doing today concerning the abortion issue is the same thing you would have done regarding slavery. Why? Because they are the same issues at the philosophical level: personal devaluation, selfishness, and utilizing other people for your own selfish gains and means. Slavery and abortion reveal the same motivations, the same philosophies at work. All things being equal, whatever kind of person you are today is the kind of person you'd have been then. Only pride would have us imagine otherwise.

The Root Causes of Pride

THE EMOTIONAL ROOT OF PRIDE IS SELF-REJECTION.
Do you feel like you do not quite measure up? I'm not asking if you have blown God's will for your life, due to your sin. I know you have. I'm asking whether you think you are worth the sacrifice Jesus made for you. Do you know why God loves you so much? If not, you have a problem with self-rejection.

God doesn't love you just because "God is love." He loves you because, being love, He knows how to appreciate the unique person that you are. The attributes that you may think of as making you worth less, God sees as making you worth more! For some reason God wanted me to have a turned up nose, flat feet, and knees that lock back too far. He had a purpose in making me color-blind, introverted, and artistically handicapped. He is not disappointed in me for these things. Just the opposite; they qualify me for unique purposes, and make me more appealing to Him. He also values my "better" qualities, but only in combination with my "worse" qualities. They work together to make me very attractive to God.

Some of my attributes (intelligence, talents, abilities), God expects me to develop. Some are simply not that important to Him. He may expect you to develop your singing voice; I think He enjoys mine just the way it is. He may expect you to take art classes; I think He wants me to draw nothing but stickmen. You see, we don't have to be good at everything for God to enjoy everything about us. Self-acceptance is having the humility to accept love for who we are, while staying committed to developing into the person God wants us to be.

Do you have self-acceptance?

THE RELATIONAL ROOT OF PRIDE IS DEPENDENCE ON THE APPROVAL OF OTHERS. We see this in relationships that are overly emotionally invested in each other (refer to the 51% Principle, Stickman Theology, chapter 7). When one person depends on another (or others) to determine whether they are good Christians or good spouses or good parents or good employees, they are motivated by pride. When we are confident in God's love, we can be more open and can stand the criticism or rejection of others. If their criticism of us is accurate, we know that God has provided for our forgiveness and redemption. If their criticism of us is inaccurate, we know that God is still at work completing his purposes for our life. We don't have to have their approval.

Most often, others' criticism of us is not condemning or rejecting but just the result of different people trying to understand each other and live together. When our emotional investment is appropriate, we do not have to defend ourselves, attack those who criticize us, or withdraw from the relationship. We can absorb the stress, anger, guilt, or hurt and call upon God to help us sort through it to determine an honest and godly response. Pride causes a reaction within us (defending, attacking, denying, or withdrawing) that makes us feel better at the moment. It causes us to sacrifice the relationship so that we can escape feelings that we won't or don't know how to live with.

THE SPIRITUAL ROOT OF PRIDE IS SELF-DEPENDENCE.

Self-dependence is evidenced by the need to come up with reasons (suitable to ourselves) to trust that we are valuable. Instead of allowing God to love us for the unique person He created us to be, we try to give Him reasons to love us. Of course, if I have something to prove, then it is up to me to prove it. When we are trying to prove ourselves (to God, to ourselves, to others) struggling, striving, and growing is not an acceptable standard. We can deal only in terms of success or failure. This forces us again into one of two alternatives: 1) denial of our weaknesses, or 2) self-rejection, thus fueling the emotional and relational roots of pride.

The apostle Paul was able to claim a heart full of love for the law of God even as he failed to fulfill the law (see Romans 7). He was able to humbly admit his failure without condemning himself by identifying himself with his heart instead of with his actions. He did not wait until his actions measured up to claim his victory in Christ! Instead, his sinful behavior served to increase his dependence on Jesus. If pride had its way in Paul at that moment, it would have insisted that He was not a good Christian. However, Paul humbled himself and embraced his need of his Savior and Redeemer with love and gratitude.

The Cure for Pride: Humility

Just before the verses we read where Jesus confronts the Pharisees, we read, "For whoever exalts himself will be humbled, and whoever humbles himself will be exalted" (Mt 23:12).

We can joyfully embrace the work of the Holy Spirit in us (refining our character), and the work of the Holy Spirit through us (utilizing all our attributes). We can trust that God is tickled silly-pink in love with us. That takes humility. We must renew our minds with the truths we have learned: We don't have to measure up to a spiritual standard of behavior. It is okay that our hearts and our minds are set on the word of God even if our characters don't measure up. That takes humility. And, we can release others from the burden of anchoring our life issues. We can give them permission to not always think that we are wonderful. That takes humility.

1) CONFESS YOUR PRIDE

Nothing hurts your sinful pride more than admitting it to those who are wounded by it. If you ever want to allow the Holy Spirit to give you victory over this sin, you must be willing to name it! Instead of telling others that their constructive criticisms are hypocritical, make you mad, or hurt your feelings, tell them the truth: your pride is hurting you so badly that you need some time alone with God to get it under control.

2) COME TO GOD AS A CHILD

The following quote is an excerpt from my book Divine Delight. I believe it is addresses this issue appropriately:

> You see, this is our argument with God. We do not want to come to Him as a child. We want a relationship of equals: adult to adult. He can't help but see us as little children in need of a wise and loving father. So, we argue with Him, we question His love for us, we doubt His wisdom in ordering our lives, we rebel against His commandments, we insist that we are able to know and do good in and of ourselves, even as we demean ourselves as His creations by having "low self-esteem." All this because we don't want to humble ourselves before Him, and simply be His children.
>
> Jesus has made it possible for us to share in a love relationship with God. However, we are not allowed to define any of the terms of the relationship. We are only allowed to accept or reject the relationship that has been offered to us: father to child. "I tell you the truth, unless you change and become like little children, you will never enter the kingdom of heaven" (Mt 18:3).

I want to encourage you to literally think of yourself as a six-year-old in the presence of God. Seek God's attention and affection like a six-year-old would. Ask Him questions, and tell Him what you want like a six-year-old would. Assume your childishness is delightful to him, because it is. When you are in the presence of God, the angels, and the saints, the only one who has any need to see you as an intellectual, moral, and capable adult is you. And that part of you is your pride.

When you come into God's presence as a child you soon realize that our love for others is tainted with selfishness. Our desire to do good is motivated by pride. Our willingness to sacrifice is a shallow pool of self-glorification. Even our desire to humble ourselves before God is marked by a need to be approved of. How difficult it is to accept ourselves as the good creation of a loving God. From somewhere deep within us comes the constant pressure to prove ourselves—to ourselves, if not to others.

It takes a conscious effort to embrace our childishness in the presence of God. Doing so is a way to open the door to the Holy Spirit to heal your sinful pride.

On the other hand, beware of approaching the presence of God in a prideful manner.

As John Piper stated in *Desiring God*: "If you come to God dutifully offering him the reward of your fellowship instead of thirsting after the reward of his fellowship, then you exalt yourself above God as benefactor and belittle him as the needy beneficiary—and that is blasphemy."

Because the father-child relationship is so vital to our walk with God, He is greatly offended when a father abuses or neglects his child. Such nurturing of the child's soul inevitably creates strongholds inhibiting the individual from embracing Father God. Jesus said that it would be better for such a "father" to tie a millstone around his neck and cast himself into the sea (see Matthew 18:6, Mark 9:42, Luke 17:2).

3) SPEAK THE TRUTH IN LOVE

Since virtues cannot simply be placed within us, circumstances must be created in which we choose to accept ourselves as we truly are. This process is commonly known as being humiliated.

Please, don't misunderstand. I am not suggesting that we reject ourselves any more than I am encouraging us to exalt ourselves. Both extremes of self-esteem (positive and negative) are a product of our pride. I am claiming that God allows us to be humiliated, hoping that we will humble ourselves; accept ourselves as His creation. I've found no better circumstance for this humbling to take place than in an accountability group with other struggling, striving, growing believers.

One clear illustration of the nature of this freedom was practiced in the renewal movement in the eighteenth-century Anglican Church that eventually became known as Methodism. Everyone who desired to be admitted to the small groups (classes) were to be asked at least seven questions. The first four had to do with the individual's salvation experience. The other three are as follows:

- Do you desire to be told your faults?
- Do you desire to be told your faults, and that plain and home?
- Consider! Do you desire we should tell you whatsoever we think, whatsoever we fear, whatsoever we hear concerning you?

Such accountability is still offered to the poor in spirit today. A friend of mine participates in an Emmaus Reunion Group. Each week they meet and hold each other accountable to their professions of Christ. They have agreed to ask and answer the questions: "Where did you participate in being the Church this week, the heartbeat of Christ?" and "When was your faith tested this week through failure?" among others. Another friend meets with his "Point-Man" accountability group where they have agreed to ask each other questions concerning several personal areas of their lives. Their final question to each other is, "Have you just lied to me?"

Only the poor in spirit (the humble) could appreciate such questions. It is true that any legalistic hypocrite could ask the questions, but the poor in spirit would not resent that.

4) ALLOW GOD TO BE GLORIFIED THROUGH YOUR FAILURES

In the kingdom of heaven, which was promised to the poor in spirit, all glory and honor belongs to our God. There is no glory or honor left to be shared with you or me within the kingdom. It all rightly belongs to God.

This is also the testimony of Charles Colson, who aided in the Nixon administration Watergate cover-up, went to prison, was saved, and now is an author and founder of Prison Fellowship. In the prologue to *Loving God*, he writes about his reflections while participating in a Prison Fellowship breakfast:

> My life of success was not what made this morning so glorious— all my achievements meant nothing in God's economy. No, the real legacy of my life was my biggest failure—that I was an ex-convict. My greatest humiliation—being sent to prison—was the beginning of God's greatest use of my life; He chose the one experience in which I could not glory for His glory."

I challenge you to share with the safe people in your life stories like Charles Colson's; in which God is glorified through your failures. Your sinful pride will not like it! By the way, if you do tell the story in a way that doesn't hurt your sinful pride, then you've told it wrong!

5) Embrace the Call to "Die to Self"

The call "to die" is not just a symbolic analogy; it is a true description of how it feels to humble ourselves. To humble ourselves feels like we are dying! And, at that moment, we must make a choice of whether we will find a way to preserve our sense of worth and escape the awkward, difficult, painful moment, or whether we will proceed through the gate of death into a lifetime of similar deaths while giving God the glory for our forgiveness and sanctification.

Take note of these humbling (humiliating) moments. Pay attention to your conditioned response (anger, withdrawal, tears, denial). Recognize your conditioned response as an effort to protect yourself from being humbled. Then, challenge yourself to not go with your conditioned response. Challenge yourself to stay in the moment of death and give yourself a chance to die to self.

Small Group Discussion

1) On a scale of one to ten (with one being very humble, and ten being very prideful) rate yourself. State why.

2. What did you learn in this chapter that was most encouraging to you?

3. Pray for each other.

Chapter Five

Sloth

When the early Church fathers spoke of the Seven Deadly Sins, they listed sloth first, as the deadliest of the Seven Deadly Sins. I chose to list pride first in order to help us gain a commitment to humility and prepare the reader for the serious self-reflection required by this study.

Each of the Seven Deadly Sins will be described and depicted in harsh terms. In doing so, I hope to depict sin as very, very ugly. By presenting the study on pride first, I planned to lay a foundation to humbly embrace God's grace to us in the midst of our sin ("But where sin increased, grace increased all the more" [Rom 5:20b]). I am not trying to uglify sin in order to uglify the person sinning; I am trying to uglify sin to let the person value himself because of the grace that has been given to us to be struggling, striving, growing Christians in the midst of our sin.

New technologies have allowed researchers of brain activity to determine that the effects of passive neglect and/or abandonment of an infant can be as debilitating long-term as aggressive physical or sexual victimization of the child.[1] The early Christian Church made even stronger statements concerning sins of omission such as neglect or abandonment, which are often related to sloth. They believed that sins of omission could be even more destructive to God's purposes than sins of commission.

---

[1] "Trauma, Attachment, and Stress Disorders: Rethinking and Reworking Developmental Issues," The Santa Barbara Graduate Institute and Center for Clinical Studies and Research and the L.A. County Early Identification and Intervention Group.
http://www.healingresources.info/trauma_attachment_stress_disorders.htm

THE DEFINITION OF SLOTH: WHEN WHAT IS IMPORTANT IS NOT WORTH THE EFFORT. I want to ask you to circle the word "important" and circle the word "effort," because these are the two sides of the coin that make sloth such a broad category. First, when what is important is not worth the effort, it may be because we have improperly defined what is important. That is why we circled "important." We could be type A personalities, go-getters, real strong energy people, task-oriented, out there just exerting all kinds of effort on the wrong things. We could be missing the priorities of God in our lives, and that would be slothful of us.

The other aspect of sloth comes about when we know what is important to God, but due to our laziness or procrastination we don't follow through. For the most part, Christians have a good idea of what their priorities should be. However, because God will forgive us, and other things seem to demand our time, or we might question our ability to succeed (or 100 other reasons), we just don't make the effort. If this sounds like you, then you have a problem with sloth.

> Then he will say to those on his left, "Depart from me, you who are cursed, into the eternal fire prepared for the devil and his angels. For I was hungry and you gave me nothing to eat, I was thirsty and you gave me nothing to drink, I was a stranger and you did not invite me in, I needed clothes and you did not clothe me. I was sick and in prison and you did not look after me." They also will answer, "Lord, when did we see you hungry or thirsty or a stranger or needing clothes or sick or in prison, and did not help you?" He will reply, "I tell you the truth, whatever you did not do for the least of these, you did not do for me." And they will go away to eternal punishment, but the righteous to eternal life.

MATTHEW 25:41–46

These are people who tried to justify their sloth. Can you imagine standing before the judgment seat in Heaven and arguing with God? These people tried to justify themselves right up to the point that God declares their eternal damnation. The slothful argued that they didn't see the need. They implied that if they had seen Jesus in need they would have helped.

(They saw themselves as acting nobly under different circumstance, evidencing an advanced degree of pride.) Jesus stated his value for "the least of these," thus shattering their attempts to justify their slothfulness.

It could seem as if these verses represent salvation being earned by works. We know that is not true. Instead, what we see here is an illustration of two things: 1) the destructiveness of sloth, and 2) a people unwilling to repent. Jesus was confronting those who had hardened their hearts against God and wouldn't repent of their motivational sin. They refused to see what was important and that it was worth the effort. These are people who were literally carried by their sloth and pride into eternal damnation. There is no place for these sins in heaven, and it seems the damned were not ready to give them up. Hell became their only option.

The Progressive Nature of Sloth

Our sin motivations are progressive in nature. The hardening of our hearts is a process. Satan will try to keep us from being self-reflective enough to discern each step of the progression, and unaware of our own hardness of heart. Then, when our sin manifestations begin, we will assume our behavior was more reactive (an uncharacteristic response to negative circumstances) than responsive (a true indication of our hardened hearts). Since we do not want to wait until we've developed a long-standing habitual sin manifestation before we consider our sin motivations, let's look at the progressive nature of sloth.

Our first step toward establishing a stronghold of sloth is to be ambivalent toward the general will of God. The general will of God refers to the desires God has for our lives that do not vary from person to person. These are the things that God wants from me, He wants from you, He wants from Jean, Joan, and Ted.

Issues such as where we go to school, what our profession is, what our ministry is, or how we manage our finances are details of conviction. Those are things that relate to the specific will of God for each of us. They When we start to question the general will of God, we are starting to deny God's authority over us. The general will of God can be compared to an operating manual. God, who created us, knows what works for and what works against us. He has given us the operating manual. When we ignore His directives, we are saying to God, "I think I know what is best for me."

In premarital counseling, the first session I spend with people is what I call "Lecture 101." In this session I educated the couple on where our loving feelings come from and how they can be maintained. During the session I explain how premarital sexual activity creates destructive elements in the marriage relationship. We discuss the negative impact of premarital sexual activity on trust, character, establishing sexual expectations, and the creation of coping mechanisms and strongholds toward each other. I usually close the session by challenging them to commit to celibacy until marriage.

More often than not, the couple tells me that they had no idea how hurtful premarital sexual activity would be to them. Many couples confess that they really thought that premarital sexual activity was helping their relationship. "This is the first time anybody has explained to us how it was hurtful to us."

My point is that we tend to put God on the hot seat and expect Him to explain, to our satisfaction, His reasons for the principles He calls us to. And God might well say, "I can't explain to you why every directive I've given you is for your own good. You are too limited to understand. Even if you could understand, why don't you just trust me?"

The first step of sloth is ambivalence toward the general will of God. The second level of slothfulness begins when we begin devaluing our God-given life purposes. For instance, I can tell myself that it doesn't matter if I am a good brother. I am the eldest child in our family. I have a tendency, and I am confessing sin here, to think that I really don't need to be that involved in my brothers' and sisters' lives. They are adults. They make their own decisions. I don't need to initiate our conversations. They know I care about them. If they want to come around, I am glad to see them. This attitude is sin on my part. One of my life purposes is to be a big brother. I have a tendency to devalue that. Slothfulness begins with devaluing, then devaluing leads to distraction. Everything else just crowds into our lives, and the best things get lost in the midst of the good things. Since good is the worst enemy of best, I miss out on God's best for me.

Devaluing leads to distraction; distraction leads to distancing. Devaluing is the spiritual root, distraction is the emotional root (withdrawing emotional investment), and distancing is the relational root. A root system that sustains a stronghold of slothfulness is growing. Soon, reestablishing a healthier relationship with my siblings becomes a very difficult chore. Yet, since there is no real pressure to change my pattern (outside of the conviction of the Holy Spirit), I find it easier to maintain the sloth than change my pattern in this area of my life.

This pattern holds true for all our life anchors, even our most vital life anchor: our relationship with God. If we devalue our moments with God, other concerns will demand our time. Then our devaluing allows us to get distracted with the concerns of life. The concerns of life grow up like weeds and choke out the seeds of love for God that have been sown in our heart. We don't really notice the change because we are just distracted. That distraction leads to distancing, and soon we don't seem to feel the presence of God and we are not hearing His voice and are not walking in conviction. Still, we may not even notice the change. There is a part of our heart and soul that is missing, but we are not missing it because we are distanced. And then we try to act like Christians, and we are defeated. Why? Because we can't do it by ourselves. We need the power of God to live holy lives, but we are defeated because we are distanced from God. Devaluing led to distraction, distraction led to distancing, and distancing led to defeat. Eventually, our defeats can lead to depression and death.

There is a notion that I want to leave with you. When my children were young I would read to them while they ate their breakfast before school each morning. When they were eight and nine years old I read to them *The Chronicles of Narnia* by C.S. Lewis. In one of the books there is a chapter called "The Deplorable Word." The deplorable word is a word that, when spoken by the evil queen, destroyed all life on her planet. For generations and generations the kings and queens had known this deplorable word, but no one had ever imagined actually speaking it. The evil queen rebelled against the rightful rule of her sister. Her sister's forces were winning the war. So, the evil queen spoke the deplorable word and wiped out all life on her planet. The book never said what the deplorable word was.

Yet, in our struggle against sloth, I know what the deplorable word is. The deplorable word is "just," as in "no big deal," as in "I was just doing this" or "I just needed to do that." "Just" is the deplorable word that can suck us into death (spiritually, relationally, and emotionally) of God's purposes in our lives. This word implies that whatever I am doing is not of value or importance. It implies that nothing of emotional, relational, or spiritual significance is happening at the moment. This is an attitude in which sloth grows.

The third level in the progression of slothfulness is lack of knowledge of or surrender to the specific will of God.

God has a specific will for your life. He created you uniquely to fulfill specific purposes. There are just too many important, good things for us to try to do that we can get lost in and lose the best. Since often we can't figure out which are the good things and which are the best, we need God to tell us.

When I was in seminary, we used to say we were going to do something for God, even if it was just making mistakes. We thought we were being really spiritual, and in a sense we were. We were saying we were not going to be sucked into sloth; we were not going to end up just not trying. We were going to continue to try. And that was the good part. But then we would say, "even if it is just making mistakes." Of course, we will make our share of mistakes, but we need to know what God wants for us. We were all at seminary because God had found a way to make it clear to us that He wanted us there. Surely, we could trust that He would continue to lead us.

In John 15:15, in part of "the high priestly prayer" Jesus prayed for his disciples on the night of his crucifixion, he said, "I no longer call you servants, because a servant does not know his master's business. Instead, I have called you friends, for everything that I learned from my Father I have made known to you."

This is Jesus' nature toward me; He wants to tell me what His will and purpose is. I won't always understand it, but He wants to tell me.

And so we come to these two primary principles for living within God's specific will.

First, God's specific will is always found within the practice of God's general will. In other words, we cannot ignore the general will of God and still think that we are fulfilling God's specific will for our lives.

I can't tell you how often I counsel with Christian people who think they are fulfilling God's purposes for their lives even though they are not studying God's word, or in submission to any godly authority, or otherwise embracing God's general will for their lives. The arrogance amazes me. Some Christians seem to be waiting for God to give them a vision high enough or a calling glorious enough to make it worth their while to begin practicing the general will of God. I want to ask them (and you?) the following question: If you are not going to practice what God has revealed to us, that He wants for all of us, then why do you think God would bother to tell you His specific will for your life? If we reject the general, we are rejecting the specific. It is not likely that God would waste His time or yours by revealing His specific will for your life when you have been unwilling to commit yourself to His general will for your life.

Second, when God chooses to reveal His specific will for your life, it is His responsibility to speak clearly. It is your responsibility to say yes. One of the questions I have been asked most often during my ministry is how to learn the specific will of God. There are principles that apply to knowing God's specific will: if it lines up with godly experience, if it lines up with your spiritual mentors, if it lines up with the general principles of God, then you are headed in the right direction. This is true, but it remains God's job to clearly communicate His specific will to you. Do not take all the responsibility on yourself, thinking that you have to become a spiritual giant with huge spiritual ears in order to hear the "still, small voice of God." No, God can speak loudly and clearly. You just have to prepare yourself to be willing to say yes.

Maybe you have seen the plaque or poster that says, "UGOTTAN-ODAONEDATMADEYA." Do you know what this says? It is communicating a biblical truth. What if I told you that, as a Christian, you should be able to decipher that message? I think a lot of Christians believe that God makes them try to figure out His confusing messages. It doesn't work that way. Instead, God tells us what He wants for us, even though the circumstances concerning how it will happen may require a lot of faith. He tells you the message directly: You gotta know the one that made you. You look at the circumstances of life and you see UGOTTANODAONEDAT-MADEYA. Then, you have to walk in faith, believing that eventually the circumstances will line up with the clear message you've been given. Once you have walked through the circumstances, you can look back and see that the message was in the circumstances also, not before.

I have been unable to find a single example in scripture where the disciples were made responsible for hearing God's voice. The message of the biblical examples is that, once God clearly communicates His will to us (and He will do so using whatever methods He has to; donkeys, prophets, handwriting on the wall, etc.), the disciple must be prepared to say, "Lead me, Lord. I will follow."

In the fourth stage of slothfulness we become overcommitted to the loudest emotional needs. Since at this stage we have lost the directives we would get from following an objective vision for our lives, we are open to being directed by other means. We don't have a rational basis for decision-making, so we end up adopting subjective (emotion-based) means of decision-making.

Once we fall into subjective decision-making, we are forced to make difficult decisions, namely, whose feelings count most. Do mine count most or do yours? Or do theirs? And usually the winner is whoever can yell at me the loudest. The squeakiest wheel gets the grease. And we fall into subjective decision-making based upon emotional needs. Which leads us to relational chaos—no responsible boundaries, self-centered manipulation, guilt messages, escape, withdrawal, prohibitive conscience, victimization, controlling, scapegoating… we could go on and on. These are all behaviors common in subjective decision-making relationships. Some therapist came up with a term for these relationships, he called it "crazy making." A relationship based on subjective decision-making will feel crazy.

Without objective means of decision-making, a couple is forced to "argue for agreement." When that doesn't work, they are left with one of three options: 1) emotionally escalate and act out, 2) accommodate the other person and become bitter, or 3) withdraw from the situation and eventually withdraw from the relationship altogether. Each decision becomes a test of who loves whom, and it ends up "crazy making."

Finally, in level five, we lose the ability to self-motivate toward set objectives. In my counseling practice, I have dealt with this reality often. People tell me: "We just can't maintain our budget." "I can't seem to discipline my children consistently." "I can't stick to this diet." "We want to go to church, but something always happens." "I don't know how to deal with sexual obligation toward my husband (or sexual sacrifice toward my wife, or vice versa)." "I can't seem to control what I say, and I can't seem to honor a timeout." The individual is saying that they are losing the ability to maintain their objectives. Their feelings are leading their train. They may think that their problem is with anger, or with pride, but in truth, they have been ensnared by sloth.

The Root Causes of Sloth

We have already discussed the elements that go into creating a stronghold of sloth within us. Let's take a moment to place those elements in the analogy of the roots of the weed that choke out our heart of righteousness.

THE EMOTIONAL ROOT OF SLOTH IS OBLIGATION TO SUBJECTIVE CARING.
Like most temptations, this destructive emotional pattern often comes disguised as an angel of light. For instance, if your church needs a Sunday school teacher for the second graders, the pastor may make a plea to the congregation. Since you are available and capable of teaching second graders, maybe you should volunteer. After all, they need you; someone was there for you when you were in second grade, and everyone else is overworked already. On the other hand, you homeschool your kids and are with them all week. You need a break. You already volunteer with Bible class on Wednesday nights. Yet, the need is there, and you will feel guilty if you don't meet it. This is the kind of thinking that characterizes those obligated to subjective caring.

There are objective alternatives. I think it is okay to say that if God doesn't raise up a person with a passion for a ministry, then maybe the church is not meant to have that ministry. No matter how badly we think the ministry is needed, it simply may not be available. For whatever reason, and we don't always have to know the reason, it is not available to us. Now we can be sad. It doesn't have to be I am bad or you are bad. It may just be we are not going to have a second grade at the church. We are going to have to decide if we are going to put them with the first graders or put them with the third graders. It may have to work even if it is a sad situation.

THE RELATIONAL ROOT OF SLOTH IS MISPLACED PRIORITIES.
Probably the most lamented manifestation of sloth among Christians is that the husband is not fulfilling his calling to be "the spiritual head of the household." I understand how overwhelming this temptation can be. Recently, our family had to deal with a crisis with one of our sons. It took five days before I could (would) pray with my wife about it. There were so many pressures to subjective decision-making, and neither of us knew for certain what we should do, so I withdrew. I did only what needed to be done, and resented being put in the situation. Instead of giving all my concerns to Jesus, I just wanted to escape them. It was amazing how clear things became for me when I began to call on Jesus. He ministered to my feelings and gave me a clear sense of direction. (Not because I was so spiritually sensitive, but because I had finally agreed to say yes to whatever He wanted.) What Jesus wanted from me first was to follow His general will; ask my wife's forgiveness for my anger and to pray with her. Then, He directed me in some specific ways. That's the way it works.

THE SPIRITUAL ROOT OF SLOTH IS THE TEMPTATION TO BE LUKEWARM CHRISTIANS.
In Revelation 3:15–16, Jesus speaks to Christians saying, "I know your deeds, that you are neither cold nor hot. I wish you were either one or the other! So, because you are lukewarm—neither hot nor cold—I am about to spit you out of my mouth."

Lukewarm Christians tend to petition God when things are difficult and give thanks to God when circumstances are good. In other words, they assume that God is there and God is active and God is trying to bless them, and they are not even aware of how lukewarm their relationship with God is. And so they say I have these needs, and so I am going to go pray to God for this or that, and maybe it happens and maybe it doesn't. And they actually think they are living out a relationship with God when, really, they are just going about their business and God is basically just letting them. Maybe God will choose to exercise discipline and hope they will recognize it as discipline; maybe He will exercise kindness and hope they recognize it as kindness. But see, with lukewarm Christians, you are almost in a no-win situation. If you act severely toward them, they say, "Oh, my life is difficult; God, please help me."

God responds, "You don't understand; I am causing this problem. I am really behind this, allowing these things to happen. I wanted you to lose your job so maybe you would start depending upon Me."

"Well, I am, God. I am asking You for another job."

"No, you don't understand; I am talking about depending on Me for more eternally significant things than your job. I was just using your job for a springboard to try and get you to address this motivational issue."

And the slothful, lukewarm Christian replies, "That's well and good, Lord, but at the moment I'm a little preoccupied with how I'm going to provide for my family. Are You going to get me a job or are You not?"

Or God can be kind and get them a job.

The slothful say, "Oh, look what God did for me."

And God says, "Well, no. I was trying to show you that I could provide for you above and beyond what you thought. I have plans for you that require that you trust me, so I gave you a better job."

Again the slothful, lukewarm Christian replies, "Thanks God, I'm very grateful. To You be the glory, You know. But, I'm kinda busy with this new job You gave me right now."

Of course, these conversations may not be conducted at a conscious level, yet they still can be lived out consistently and persistently.

The Cure for Sloth: Developing Diligence

Begin at step one and recommit to the general will of God for your life. Repent of your slothfulness. Establish the lifestyle of a struggling, striving, growing believer (see chapter 12). Be faithful in little things. Reclaim your priorities.

Set objectives in life purposes. Repent when you fail. And trust that God is transforming your life, beginning where His love and wisdom dictate.

1)   I want to emphasis the challenge to trust that God is transforming your life, beginning where He wants to begin.

All too often, we want to dictate the process and tell God where we want Him to begin. "God, I have to decide if I am going to OSU or OU. Begin at this point in Your relationship with me, God. Tell me which one You want me to go to."

And, God is saying, "I don't care if you go to OU or OSU. What I want is to struggle with you about this relationship with your parents. That is My concern right now. So, I want you to go wherever your parents think is best. I think it is important that you take this chance to honor your father and your mother one last time before you leave home."

When we recommit ourselves to Him, His love and His wisdom will dictate what areas of our lives we address in relationship with Him first. We don't get to dictate to God where we start in our relationship with Him.

Ask God in which area of your life He wants to challenge your sinful sloth. Keep asking until you believe you have an answer. Don't give up on gaining a clear sense of God's guidance in this struggle. Don't guess what God wants to do in you; ask and wait, ask and wait, ask and wait. This is the first step in challenging your sinful sloth.

Godly diligence is more than just working hard at good things. We can appear to be diligent while setting our own priorities and pursuing our own goals. Don't be fooled by this façade. The hardest working people you know may still be the most slothful.

As soon as you have a sense of which area of your life God wants to use to heal your sinful sloth, tell your safe people about it. This is important; don't neglect it!

2)   Adapt an attitude of importance: Your gifting and calling are of the utmost importance to the kingdom.

I have recently asked two large groups of believers to think about those who have impacted their lives for the better and to determine who among all the people they know seem to be most important to the kingdom of

God. Each group had several participants that offered their answers. None gave the answer I was looking for. I was hoping someone would say that of all the people they know that they themselves seemed most important to the kingdom of God. I believe that this is the answer God would encourage each of us to give. Hang with me. I know this sounds like I'm promoting arrogance, but I truly am not. I am promoting a joyful embracing of the passions and giftings God has given you. It is a fact of our human condition that we can appreciate the giftings and passions of others but can only experience the passions and giftings God has given us.

In other words, we should each be doing whatever it is that God has put in our hearts. The preacher should carry a passion for illustrating and applying God's word to our current culture. The youth minister should believe that the future lies in the hands of our youth. Fathers and mothers should believe that they are shaping the world through their example and their children. Husbands and wives should believe that they are demonstrating to the world the love that Christ has for the Church. Each believer should believe that they are of utmost importance to the kingdom of God. "To each one the manifestation of the Spirit is given for the common good." (1 Cor 12:7)

Let me share with you a paradox (two things that seem contradictory but actually reveal a higher truth): The more you value your own passions and giftings, the more you will value those of others. You will find that embracing an attitude of importance does not place you above others, but instead increases your dependence on and appreciation of the passions and giftings of others. Recognizing your value as a member of the Body increases your love for the Body as a whole.

I've known many people who have become frustrated with the church and have withdrawn from it. I've heard people with a gift of service complain that twenty percent of the people do eighty percent of the work. I've heard people with a gift of compassion say that the church ignores the wounded and hurting people in their midst. I've heard the preachers and teachers assert that others don't love God's word like they should. In other words, we get offended when others are not like us. This is not because we value our passions and giftings too highly; it is because we place such a low value on our passions and giftings that we actually think everyone should have them. We tend to believe that our passions and giftings should be common, not special. So we end up demeaning ourselves by thinking of our passions and giftings as common and demeaning others by thinking they should be more like us. The truth is that the more highly we value our own passions and giftings, the more we will appreciate those of others. And, we will stop expecting others to be like us. Diligence requires that we know the value of what we have to offer.

3)   Most importantly, you must know the purpose of your job!

Regardless of your spiritual giftings, your ministry roles, and your life purposes, your God-given job is to enjoy God, enjoy yourself, and enjoy others.

"God is not unjust; he will not forget your work and the love you have shown him as you have helped his people and continue to help them. We want each of you to show this same diligence to the very end, in order to make your hope sure" (Heb. 6:10-11).

According to this verse, our diligence and our hope go hand in hand. Our diligence to love and serve others confirms our hope that God loves and serves us, and vice versa. If we serve others out of a sense of duty or in order to earn God's approval, then our view of God will be the same— that He serves us out of His sense of duty rather than His love for us. That view of God does not inspire my desire to be with Him eternally. Similarly, your service to others must spring from a heart of love for them in order to qualify as diligence in God's eyes.

The reason for this is simple; your sense of duty will not move you to the depths of intimacy and connection that God's purposes require. Duty will never touch the soul of another human being.

It is not enough to avoid sloth. God desires that we diligently love and serve others from the same motivation that he diligently loves and serves us. Paul gave thanks over and over, in epistle after epistle, for "your work produced by faith, your labor prompted by love, and your endurance inspired by hope in our Lord Jesus Christ" (1 Thes 1:3). Just as the diligent give thanks for each other today.

Small Group Discussion

1) On a scale of one to ten (with one being very diligent and ten being very slothful) rate yourself. State why.

2) If you struggle with sloth, are you more likely to improperly define what is important or to not put out the effort to do what you know is important?

3) Who is the most diligent person you know? What makes you think so?

4) Pray for each other's struggle against sloth.

Chapter Six

Lust

"You cannot prevent the birds from flying over your head. But let them only fly and do not let them build a nest in the hair of your head."

MARTIN LUTHER

Our definition of lust for this chapter: exaggerating or denying the spiritual significance of someone or something.

Lust is most commonly associated with sexual sin, but not limited to it. Since being sexually motivated or sexually excited is not necessarily a sin, we will describe lust as the point where we cross the line in inappropriately nurturing our sensual (as opposed to spiritual) perspective concerning people and things. As with each of our other sin motivations, the line between where natural responses become sinful responses is hard to define. We usually do not live on one side of the line or the other, but sometimes straddle the line, sometimes make short trips back and forth across it, and may not realize when we have actually set up camp on the bad side of it.

Denying Spiritual Significance

The line involving lust has to do with whether or not we are recognizing the true spiritual significance of a person or a thing. Sometimes the line seems fairly easy to define, as in the case of pornography. Pornography is an intentional effort to focus on the sensual and exclude the spiritual. I doubt that many men really care about Miss September's personality, intelligence, or hopes for the future. The purpose of pornography is to strip

Miss September of more than her clothes. It is to strip her of her spiritual significance so that the viewer can focus on her sensual aspects alone.

However, even pornography is not always clearly defined as being across the line. We are capable of putting Miss September in a see-through swimsuit and calling her a sports model, or in a see-through blouse and calling her a fashion model, or giving her a product to hold and calling her an advertising model, or positioning funny sayings in thought bubbles over her head and calling her an entertainer, even carving her in stone and calling her a work of art. Pornography can sometimes make the claim of communicating personality, intelligence, and even hope for the future. And, sometimes the claim is true. So, how much does Miss September have to cover up before she is no longer promoting lust?

You know what? It really doesn't matter. The reality is that you and I cannot blame our lust on others. No one can force us to deny their spiritual significance. "The temptation to give in to evil comes from us and only us. We have no one to blame but the leering, seducing flare-up of our own lust. Lust gets pregnant, and has a baby: sin! Sin grows up to adulthood, and becomes a real killer" (Jas 1: 14-15, *The Message*).

Yes, we can be tempted, but we can't be forced. The bird can fly over our heads. We don't have to invite it to build a nest in our hair. We can respect others, even when they are disrespecting themselves.

QUESTION: Okay, we are responsible for our own thoughts. No one can force us to reject any thoughts from a spiritual perspective. So, let's get down to where the rubber meets the road. If I see a sexy person and my heart falls into my stomach and I begin to burn inside, am I lusting?

ANSWER: Not necessarily. Our sexual longing for an attractive person is a part of how God created us. God wants us to accept ourselves as sexual beings. However, every natural need can be inappropriately nurtured. If we allow our thoughts to linger on the sensuality of a person, we are nurturing lust. If we allow our feelings (the "burning") to fade at its own rate, without nurturing it, we are not guilty of lust.

We must let our feelings be a natural signal to us that we are being tempted. Then, we must decide whether we will entertain the temptation or reject it. It may be partly your fault that you encountered the temptation (you could "keep your eyes on their eyes"). But, it is also partly the other person's fault that you are tempted (they flaunted their sensuality). And, it is also partly God's fault that you are tempted (He created you with a sex drive). However, only you can decide to nurture or reject the temptation. God is not tempting you. He understands how you feel and will help you see the spiritual significance of others if you will call on Him.

Exaggerating Spiritual Significance

Lust is not always *sexual* in nature. Lust is *sensual* in nature. There is a difference. Appealing to the senses (sensuality) is not inappropriate unless it is accompanied by a distortion or a denial of a true spiritual perspective. Sensuality accompanied by a true spiritual perspective is healthy and holy.

For example, imagine that you are watching a commercial for the most stylish sport-utility vehicle you have ever seen. The SUV is depicted in its most attractive light, sitting on a mountain peak while the sun sets. Somehow it arrived at the mountain peak without a scratch or any dirt on it. We can picture ourselves sitting in the rich leather seats, looking out through the streak-free and perfectly tinted front window, viewing this most amazing of sunsets from a perspective that only this SUV could provide us. It is a feast for our senses. We may think, "Having this car would make my life glorious." At that moment we are lusting. We have exaggerated the spiritual significance of the vehicle. This is not a true spiritual perspective.

Maybe a luxury vehicle doesn't have that kind of appeal for you. Maybe it is a house, clothes, success, education, respect, or even your job. You can attribute too much spiritual significance to anything.

We can convince ourselves that we need a person or thing to fill a void within our lives (falling in love?). Of course, God knows our needs and makes appropriate provision for them. The provision of our needs is His special domain. He asks us to trust Him, even in the midst of tribulations. Remember, Jesus was tempted to turn a stone into bread after forty days of fasting, and resisted. He is the same Jesus who exhorted us, saying, "But seek first his kingdom and his righteousness, and all these things will be given to you as well" (Mt 6:33). Only someone whose temptations have been greater than mine has a right to advise me on how to face mine. And,

I have to admit, I think Jesus' temptation was much more difficult than mine. I think I should take His advice. Don't you?

The Progressive Manifestations of Lust

For since the creation of the world God's invisible qualities—his eternal power and divine nature—have been clearly seen, being understood from what has been made, so that men are without excuse. For although they knew God, they neither glorified him as God nor gave thanks to him, but their thinking became futile and their foolish hearts were darkened. Although they claimed to be wise, they became fools and exchanged the glory of the immortal God for images made to look like mortal man and birds and animals and reptiles. Therefore God gave them over in the sinful desires of their hearts to sexual impurity for the degrading of their bodies with one another. They exchanged the truth of God for a lie, and worshiped and served created things rather than the Creator—who is forever praised. Amen.

ROMANS 1:20-25

1)   An Unwillingness to Experience God Through Nature

First, since the creation of the earth, God's invisible attributes have been seen through the creation. So a first manifestation of lust is this: simply an unwillingness to experience God through nature. God is there to meet us in the midst of nature (with or without the new SUV). There is a spiritual significance to just walking outside and enjoying the sunshine. And God wants hearts that are willing to see spiritual significance in the natural order of things. So we are beginning to identify with God's created purpose, God's assigned values to the nature of our world. And it starts with creation—just simply saying, "God, You are here. I witness you in the blessing of the created order."

Let me give you an example of how we can exaggerate or deny this. Let's take animals. Let's *take* cats…. That's my idea; just *take* them wherever you want to, put them in a bag, throw them in a deep hole! What is that? That is denial of the spiritual significance of cats. I am confessing sin on my part. There is something about me that is unwilling to see the nature of

God within His created order. And so I don't allow myself the blessing of experiencing God in the nature of a cat.

I know I have upset some of you by demonstrating my sinful attitude in devaluing cats. For those of you I didn't offend, let me give another illustration, this time using dogs. This illustration comes from the opposite extreme.

I have actually heard people confess to sin without realizing it. They have said something like, "We've got this dog. And this dog is a member of the family, and it loves us and we love it back. And, you know, it is just like a child to us. It got sick and now we are spending $250 a month on these little pills to keep it alive. But, the dog has been so faithful and brave, we can't put it to sleep until after our daughter leaves for college." They have endowed this dog with a sense of personality beyond its true attributes. They have exaggerated its spiritual significance. They have elevated the dog to the significance and commitments due to family.

Therefore, lust can go both ways. We can exaggerate spiritual significance or we can deny it.

2)   Not Honoring God as God

In verse 21, Paul claims that, though they saw God and knew God, they did not honor Him as God. So a second manifestation of lust is to not honor God as God.

I have a pastor friend who keeps a plaque on his desk that reads, "There is a God and you are not Him." He recognizes our ability to go about life as if we know what we are doing. The truth of the matter is that we don't know what we are doing. And, even if we did know, we are not capable of doing it without God. Yet, day after day we go about our business as if we didn't need God. We plan, we work, we eat, we sleep, and we talk about it all, without an ounce of dependence on God…unless we reach a crisis, or we go to worship, or it is time to say our prayers. Then, we pull God out of His little box. We repeat the right words that make Him work. When everything turns out okay, we tell ourselves that we have faith. If it doesn't all work out okay, we wonder why God failed us. We acknowledge God, but do not honor Him as God.

This dynamic of lust is almost universal in its appeal to American Christians. I call it "the denial of the spiritual significance of the Spirit." I know it sounds corny, but it's true. For the most part, American Christians don't think that the spiritual is a very significant part of our lives. We tend to think of our sensual reality as the place where everything of importance happens and that the spiritual realm plays a part in it. However, scripture says, "Repent, for the kingdom of God is near" (Mt 3:2, 4:17), proclaiming that the spiritual realm is where everything of importance happens, and we are invited to play a part in it.

This is the good news. We are invited to be a part of God's plans. We don't deserve such an honor, but He loves us and has decided to make us a part of His eternal purposes.

3) Becoming Futile in our Thinking

The scripture goes on to say they did not honor him and they became futile in their speculations and their foolish hearts were darkened. So, a third manifestation of lust is uncertainty concerning the nature, character, and purposes of God. So when we begin to lust, we start to raise issues like this: I just really don't know if God loves me. I don't really know why He loves me. I really don't think God has much of a purpose for my life. I really don't know if God is really a loving, kind God. We begin revisiting questions that have already been answered for us within the self-revelation of God through nature, scripture, experience, and the incarnation. Sometimes we can ask these as honest questions. At other times, it is just futile thinking and an exercise in lust.

4) Filling our "God-Shaped Hole" with People and Things

The fourth step: After becoming foolish and futile in their speculations and foolish in their hearts, it says they exchanged the glory of the incorruptible God for an image in the form of corruptible man, birds, and creatures. Once we have disqualified God from meeting our needs as He sees fit (by dishonoring Him and becoming futile in our thinking) we have to find something to make us feel loved and valuable.

However, since we have already rejected true spirituality as the means to meet our needs, what avenues are left to us? Actually, there are two: first, to seek a false spirituality (mysticism, demonism, pantheism, etc.) or second, to seek our fulfillment in sensuality. Either of these options inevitably transitions into the final manifestation of lust.

5)   Demeaning and Dishonoring Ourselves

Verse 24: "Therefore God gave them over in the sinful desires of their hearts to sexual impurity for the degrading of their bodies with one another."

Let me be clear about this. What do you think is happening at the relational level when a couple practices "swinging" (trading partners with another couple for a night of sex)? I can tell you, because I have counseled a number of couples who have been through it.

The swingers are trading any honor, trust, intimacy, and respect they may have for each other for the temporary sensual pleasure of being accepted, affirmed, and pleasured. No one feels more confident in the relationship or more content afterwards.

You may be familiar with the cliché about "trading your soul to the devil." In a very real sense, that is what this last stage of lust is about. There is a trade being made. Inappropriate sensual pleasures come at the cost of spiritual blessings. Although the sensual and the spiritual are meant to find their fulfillment together in the principles of God, lust insists that you pursue the sensual at the cost of the spiritual.

Let me give a less extreme example. A highschool student told me that he had taken a date to see the movie Titanic. I said, "Wow, there was some nudity and sex scenes in that movie. Was that uncomfortable for you or your date?"

"No," he answered. "It was no big deal."

"You mean when you got excited it wasn't embarrassing for you or your date?"

"I didn't get excited. It was just part of the movie."

The young man thought I would appreciate the fact that he didn't get excited viewing the nudity and sex scenes. Instead, I told him that it really concerned me that he didn't get excited. I told him that God created him to be strongly affected by just the sight of the female body. That he was able to watch a sex scene without his "sex motivations" kicking into high gear meant that his God-given "response mechanism" was somehow not fully functioning.

That most Christians would prefer our youth to "not be affected" by nudity is an indication of how focused we are on sin manifestations, and how ignorant we are of sin motivations. Believe me, God is much more concerned with our motivations. The fact that the young man was not affected by what he saw (if it is true) is indication that the bird (lust) had made some progress in building its nest in his hair.

A Final Illustration

A fairly wealthy older couple came for counsel concerning their children. Their children were in their mid-thirties. The couple told of how their children lived beyond their means financially, and expected their parents to support their lifestyles. The parents felt used. They were upset that their children didn't have better values concerning money management. Then the couple assured me that they were not concerned about the money they gave their children. They were concerned about their children. "Our money, our houses, our cars—they don't mean anything to us. We are not concerned about that. We are just concerned about the kids."

"Oh, so that's where your children get their lust for money. You taught it to them."

"No, no, you must have misunderstood," they replied. "We said that the money means nothing to us."

"That's what I thought you said. And, you have just made a confession of lust." I explained to them that their cars and money and homes have a spiritual significance and purpose. It should have meant a great deal to them that God entrusted them with the amount of money they had. I explained that their children were using money however they saw fit, just like their parents. Even though the parents argued that they had been very responsible money managers, I pointed out that they still thought of the money as theirs to use as they saw fit. The fact that they inappropriately "tried to be generous toward their children" did not change the fact that they all had denied the spiritual significance of money. I assured them that

God did not intend for them to use "their" money to buy their children's favor, any more than God approved of their children's lavish lifestyles. I explained that the couple was showing the same attitude toward God as their children were showing toward them as parents.

This couple chose to ask their children's forgiveness for setting them the example of lusting after money. They explained to their children that they no longer considered their money to be theirs but God's. Therefore, they would try to manage it as God would have them to, which did not include supporting their children's indulgences. The children forgave their parents, and both also asked for forgiveness and committed to respecting the spiritual significance of money. The older son is now working as an investment analyst and financial consultant. He considers his job to be a ministry.

The Root Causes of Lust

The emotional root of lust is misidentifying the needs within us.

"This *will* give me the joy that I am looking for, or at least a break from the pain/boredom/guilt/hopelessness."

We may not voice such a thought out loud (actually, some do), but we think it. And, in doing so, we have honestly misidentified our needs. Our greatest needs are all spiritual ones. Our sense of value, our sense of purpose, our sense of power, and the character to use those to glorify God— those are our greatest needs. God can and will meet these needs as well as others.

It is also very important to take note that our Christian culture tends to be very uncomfortable acknowledging legitimate sexual motivations. When we are unable to discuss our sexuality as a natural part of ourselves, we are training ourselves to lust. Our inhibitions toward acknowledging God-given sexual motivations create a need to exaggerate or deny our own spiritual significance. If we cannot talk openly and honestly about our sexuality, we are denigrating a part of ourselves that God intended us to enjoy. Then we are left to the idea that sexual fulfillment is heaven itself (spiritual exaggeration) or not important at all to the spiritually mature (spiritual denial).

Let me issue a challenge in this regard. I challenge you to have a conversation with your spouse or with a trusted friend about masturbation. "Masturbation" is not a cussword. I'm not asking you to reach agreements about the biblical guidelines concerning masturbation. I'm only asking that you use this topic to get in touch with any inhibitions you may have about sexuality in general.

THE RELATIONAL ROOT OF LUST IS OUR WILLINGNESS TO
USE OTHERS TO MEET OUR NEEDS.

When we reject a true spiritual perspective of ourselves and of our lives, we become dependent on people or things to confirm our value. Often, their words (like God's words) are not enough. We need to be shown that we are valued. For those who have found sexual activity to be a means of feeling affirmed (in reality or in fantasy) their temptation will be to use others to meet this emotional need. They will be drawn to pornography or more direct sexual contact with others.

I have been asked by more than one spouse of a sexual addict, "Why doesn't he think I'm enough for him?" Part of the answer to that question is always the fact that since the spouse knows the addict and doesn't always affirm them, the sexual addict's activity with their spouse does not meet their need for the affirmation they get in their fantasy relationships.

Let me take just a moment to point out that every relationship that includes sexual activity outside of marriage is a fantasy relationship. Whether it is premarital sexual activity, pornography, strip clubs, or prostitutes, the relationship is not one based on trust and commitment; it is a fantasy relationship. Even married people are tempted to masturbation just because it is emotionally and relationally easier than engaging their spouse; they are drawn to a fantasy relationship.

The other side of this issue is our inability to receive sexual comfort from our spouse, or their inability to offer it. If sex is limited to a set pattern of touching and kissing, or if our lovemaking is limited to highly romantic dynamics, then there are inhibitions in effect. The same is true if the spouse with higher sexual motivation or the spouse with lower sexual motivation is judged by the other. Neither spouse's level of sexual motivation is wrong, and neither carries obligations for the couple. Each individual is responsible for how they conduct themselves sexually, whether it is the spouse with the higher motivations' ability to limit themselves or the spouse with the lower motivations' willingness to offer themselves. If these responsibilities are not embraced, then there is a relational root of lust in the marriage.

THE SPIRITUAL ROOT OF LUST IS DENIAL OF YOUR PERSONAL VALUE.

Each of the five manifestations of lust are born out of our denial of our own spiritual significance. To not believe that God has a wonderful, powerful, fulfilling, and eternally significant plan for your life is not just demeaning to God. It is demeaning to you. You are a spiritual being. You are an eternal being. The most important needs you have are spiritual ones. The most incredible things about you are derived from the knitting together of your body and your spirit to create a unique soul. To deny the value of the spiritual is to deny the value of your own soul. Therefore, lust is an attack upon your personal value: "Do you not know that your bodies are members of Christ himself?" (1 Cor 6:15a). Those who can't answer this question affirmatively, and those who ignore this question, have developed a spiritual root of lust.

The Cure for Lust: Love and Passion

FIRST, reclaim your own spiritual value, and believe in God's love for you. Let God love you! You have to know in your innermost being that God is not waiting for you to get things right before He offers himself in love to you. Scripture goes so far as to say "we love because he first loved us" (1 Jn 4:19). This is not implying that He loved us five times and now we ought to love Him back at least once or twice. What it means is if we receive His love, His love changes us and we love Him back. But the issue is whether or not we will receive it. Will we let God love us?

SECOND, bring your needs to God and let your passions explode. C. S. Lewis claimed that the problem God has with us is not that our passions are too large but that they are too small. Whose idea was it that we should want to "live life to the fullest," and what does that mean? Well, to the

Christian, it means wanting to change the nature of the world. I want to be used to impact eternity. Is that arrogant and egotistical? No, that is being excited about the purposes that God created me for and the "good works, which God prepared in advance for us to do" (Eph 2:10) to affect all of eternity. But the thing is, when you hear the commercial that says go for the gusto, you say no, we have to rein in that passion. Wrong! We have got to explode far beyond the gusto. The gusto is not enough; I want to affect eternity.

Our passions are too small. When we start allowing our passions to explode, we know the fulfillment of them can only be found in God and in the promises of God. At the height of my sexual ecstasy with my wife (and you don't have to blank any of this out; this is all appropriate and acceptable), I want to take her body and literally just pull it into myself. I want to blend and merge and belong with her and to her and her with me and to me. That is what I want. You know what? I can't do that anywhere with anybody in this lifetime. But that is still what I want. And you know what? I think I am going to have that. I don't know for sure how things happen in heaven, but I think we are going to be able to hug and to embrace and to blend into each other. I think we are going to somehow be able to be a part of each other and to exchange essences of encouragement from the depths of our souls, and to come away encouraged and enlivened and invigorated for having met together.

You may say that idea is all speculation. I know. There is no theological strength to it, except God has made promises to us beyond our imaginations, so why don't we let our imaginations run wild? It is not that our imaginations are going to exceed what God has created for us. We are just going to be getting close if we let our imaginations run. So we let our passions explode.

FINALLY, the cure for lust is to love others. Love is agreeing with God's given spiritual value of a person or thing (the antithesis of lust). Love is not something we work ourselves up to. It is something we allow God to show us. If we are willing to see the spiritual value of a person, we will find ourselves loving them. If we are willing to see the spiritual value of anything, then we will be able to use it lovingly. (As the saying goes, you will love things and use people, or you will use things in loving people.)

I worked with one young man who claimed that he could never seek sexual favors from the same person twice because once he knew them as a person he could never bring himself to demean them again. Although his sin was rampant, he may be nearer to victory over his lust than others who would never act out in the ways he has.

Love Others as You Love Yourself

If you are able to love yourself as a sexual being (self-acceptance), you will be able to love (not lust after) other sexual beings. If you are able to believe that God is tickled-silly-pink in love with you just the way you are, you will be able to appropriately value others just the way they are. If you are able to value God's purposes for your life, you will be able to value God's purposes for others despite how different they are.

Small Group Discussion

1) On a scale of one to ten (with one being very loving and ten being very lustful) rate yourself. State why.

2) Who is the most loving person you know? What makes you think so?

3) Pray for each other's struggle against lust.

Chapter Seven

Greed

The definition of greed: claiming that we have greater needs (physical and material) than others.

I often present couples I counsel with the challenge of rating themselves and their spouses in each of the Seven Deadly Sins. I can't remember a time when anyone rated themselves or their spouse high in the category of greed. I would guess that if I averaged each of the categories of sin motivations reported by those I have asked, the other six sin motivations would all average out about the same (approximately a six), whereas the average given to greed would be about half that given to the others (approximately a three).

I do not think this is a result of seeing a group of people who happened to actually be less affected by greed than most. I believe this result is accounted for in that our culture is so deeply saturated by greed that we have difficulty identifying when and how we are being affected by it. In other words, we really have no idea what life without greed would really look like. We may have some understanding of generosity (the antithesis of greed) as an attitude and an action, but no understanding of generosity as a lifestyle.

For the most part, the American Church has offered no alternative to our understanding of biblical stewardship that is not bound to the liberal or conservative political agendas. Whether it is through taxes or tithes, aiding the disadvantaged or presenting the gospel, the financing of our goals through agencies, institutions, and representatives is still the primary means of generosity promoted. We support ministries, send missionaries, and endow institutions. The more money we give, the more generous, and less greedy, we consider ourselves. Yet, we may have yet to touch on the true nature of greed or generosity.

Greed has the power to affect one's soul, even when one is outwardly manifesting generosity. It is that matter of the soul that concerns us. Jesus set an example for us of looking past the "surface issues" and into the heart.

One such example, concerning greed, is recorded for us in Luke 12:13–21. One of the multitude said to Jesus, "'Teacher, tell my brother to divide the inheritance with me.' Jesus replied, 'Man, who appointed me a judge or an arbiter between you?'"

Jesus is asking the man, "Are you sure you want Me to be a judge in this matter? Do you have any idea what My presuppositions or My values are in the matter of money?" And then He goes on to say: "'Watch out! Be on your guard against all kinds of greed; a man's life does not consist in the abundance of his possessions.'"

And then Jesus told the parable of the man whose harvests were so great that he tore down his barns to build bigger ones, and was confronted by God saying, "'You fool! This very night your life will be demanded from you. Then who will get what you have prepared for yourself?'"

The point Jesus is making is hard for American Christians to hear. Jesus concludes His conversation by saying, "'This is how it will be with anyone who stores up things for himself but is not rich toward God.'" And, American Christians take this to mean: It is okay to store up things for ourselves as long as we support God's work (give money to our local church, missions, and ministries). And we miss Jesus' point. Maybe we miss it because we can't believe what Jesus really means. So, let me state Jesus' point by imagining the young man's response to Jesus' hesitancy to become the arbiter.

"Jesus, are You trying to tell me that I might be better off without my share of the inheritance? Do You really think that having land and money could be detrimental to my soul? Jesus, You must not realize that money is a morally and spiritually neutral thing; if I use it for good, it's good, or if I use it for bad, it's bad. Obviously, I'm convinced that I would use it for good. You, however, seem to think that Mammon will have a negative effect upon my soul, whether I use it for good or not. That can't be right, can it? You aren't really saying that I would be affected by wealth the same way that guy in the parable was, are You?"

Actually, that is exactly what Jesus is saying. He worked hard to make His point, yet we still miss it, maybe because we are so poorly skilled in self-reflection that we can no longer see the obvious. Our society is the wealthiest the world has ever known, but are we more confident or less confident in God because of it? My observation is that the wealthier we become, the more confident we become in ourselves, not God.

Second, as we gain financial security, do we tend to feel more compassionate toward others or less? Again, let me answer: Although we may be better able to act compassionately toward others, the more financially secure we become the more difficult it becomes to feel compassionate toward others.

The opposite of greed is generosity. Generosity is sacrificing your wants (physical and material) in order to meet others' needs. It supposes an understanding of the power of Mammon to promote our independence from God and lack of compassion toward others. Therefore, generosity, properly exercised, is an emotional investment in callings too large for us to ever accomplish, and in people we actually know and relate to. It is freedom from greed.

The "churchy" alternative to generosity is "good stewardship." The "good stewardship" teachings I've heard tend to be derived from the Mammon-is-morally-and-spiritually-neutral philosophy. "Good stewardship" can be summarized as giving your tithes (and even some "gifts" beyond the tithe) to God, and living responsibly on the rest (minimizing debt and living within your means). It is my contention that a greedy person could practice "good stewardship" without having his or her greed inhibited. That model of stewardship *could* actually further one's independence from God and lack of compassion toward others.

A Unique Alternative to Good Stewardship: Covenant Community

In the book of Acts, chapters 2 and 4, we are given a description of covenant community. At the heart of covenant community were two basic principles: One was intimacy in relationship, the other was the sharing of liabilities.

I don't have to tell you that our local churches believe in sharing assets. Time, energy, money, gifts, and talents are assets you are called upon to "tithe," "commit," or "give" for the benefit of us all. But, covenant community is also about sharing liabilities, weaknesses, financial debt, emotional and relational needs, and so on. Covenant community is about creating a safe place for people to struggle, strive, and grow with the support of others. It's a safe place for sinners, down-and-outers, failures, the dysfunctional, the disconnected, and the ignorant.

Yet, for me, the concept of covenant community initially raised a lot of red flags. I could imagine deadbeats living off the work of others, or a dictatorial group of leaders telling everyone how much money they could spend on their wife's birthday present and what kind of car they had to drive. Actually, I don't believe that covenant community has to follow any set guidelines or rules. I think we were meant to develop the guidelines for covenant community to fit the vision of ministry that God calls us to. Yeah, I know that sounds vague, but what an adventure! Can you imagine a group of people struggling with the issues of expectations, needs, management of assets, and freedom in Christ within the context of covenant community? This is not Communism or Socialism where sharing of liabilities and assets is forced on everyone. Covenant community is a group of people volunteering willingly to embrace sharing liabilities, whether it is emotional, relational, spiritual, financial, or even physical. They are those who weep with those who weep and rejoice with those who rejoice.

I don't know exactly how each covenant community would protect itself from any "cultish" practices, but I do know that covenant community is a context in which our greed is confronted (see the story of Ananias and Sapphira in Acts 5:1-11). It seems that, although Ananias and Sapphira went above and beyond what was "fair" and what was "good stewardship," their greed was a profound sin against covenant community.

Greed

Five Manifestations of Greed

1) Evaluating Fairness Based on Distribution of Assets

In a recent presidential election, the vice-presidential candidate on the Democratic side said we should "honor our fathers and our mothers" by supporting the proposed prescription drug plan. I don't believe the candidate was trying to be flippant or manipulative. I think he really believed that my placing a vote to support a program that forces other people to pay for my parents' prescription drugs would be honoring to them. I wouldn't have to see my parents or know what they are dealing with or intrude upon their privacy to know what their finances really are, but somehow I am honoring them by voting for the right candidate and the right governmental program?

It's really a distorted way of thinking, but it is not that different from some sermons I've heard in my conservative local church. Whereas the presidential candidate wanted me to "honor my father and mother" by supporting his program, our local churches often ask us to "spread the gospel" by supporting their program. We don't have to see, talk to, or know anything about those we are "ministering to" with our tithes and offerings.

The alternative I'm promoting is only slightly different, but the slight difference makes all the difference in confronting the sin motivation of greed. Instead of giving to a church, mission, or ministry, we should give toward a vision. A vision is always larger than we will ever be capable of fulfilling, and connects us directly with people with a calling and a passion to meet needs, or the people with the needs themselves. A vision draws us to itself. We are dwarfed by it, and drawn into it. It demands a dependence on God and a connectedness to others. We don't stand outside and unaffected by the needs of others, but are drawn alongside and within the needs of others.

Without such a vision, we are left to our notions of "fairness" and our principles of "good stewardship."

2) Valuing Your Life Based on the Accumulation of Assets

What does it mean to "earn a good living"? A second manifestation of greed is valuing your life based upon the accumulation of assets. We may call it "achieving a higher standard of life" or "earning a good living," but we don't mean it in the biblical sense of proven character, clarity in our callings, and belonging to an intimate fellowship. For most of us, "a higher standard of life" simply means having more money so we can buy nicer things. We may know that the bumper sticker claiming, "He who dies with the most toys, wins" is wrong. But, for the most part, American Christians live as if it were true.

Self-esteem, social status, influence, intelligence, and even attractiveness to the opposite sex can be enhanced or harmed by your ability to make and/or manage money. Any time any of these aspects of our lives are considered to be dependent on Mammon, there is greed.

3) Stockpiling Assets

The third manifestation of greed is directing your thoughts and energies toward the stockpiling of assets. If I were to ask, "How are you set for the future?" you could answer, "Well, I'm part of the biblical community, my family is stable, I'm trusting God more and more every day, I know that God's purposes for me are being worked out step by step, and I'm looking forward to the future." Do we give that answer? Or do we say, "Well, my 401k looks like this and my retirement account looks like that"?

Someone might say, "That's not fair, Terry. You didn't tell us you were looking for a *spiritual* answer." We can all give the "churchy" answer. But, what do we really believe and live out? Do you believe that your future will be determined more by your money or your relationship with God? "Both" is not an answer, because "you cannot serve both God and Money" (Mt 6:24, Lk 16:13).

This stage of greed is about which God you serve, the Lord or Mammon. Which master has the ability to inspire your greatest efforts, make you mourn or rejoice, and give you reason for jumping out of bed in the morning?

4) Comforting Your Soul with Mammon

The fourth manifestation of greed is comforting your soul through the securing of assets. This stage of greed is about which God you trust, the Lord or Mammon. After all, money is visible, tangible, and powerful.

The Lord is invisible, intangible, and can seem anything but powerful. Which do you trust?

Greed would say, "You can trust the Lord for meaning and purpose in your life, but without cold hard cash it ain't gonna happen." Whereas, God would say, "If you trust Me for meaning and purpose in your life, you must trust *My* provision; if you try to provide for yourself, you will not fulfill My purposes." Like the hopeful disciples who were rejected by Jesus (see Luke 9:57–62), we want to get our practical concerns resolved before we can commit to follow Jesus wherever He might lead us.

5)   Resenting the Legitimate Needs of Others

The final manifestation of greed is resentment toward those who make claims upon your assets. In the book of 1 Timothy, Paul exhorts Timothy: "Command those who are rich in this present world not to be arrogant nor to put their hope in wealth, which is so uncertain, but to put their hope in God, who richly provides us with everything for our enjoyment. Command them to do good, to be rich in good deeds, and to be generous and willing to share" (1 Tm 6:17–18). But, Paul didn't understand the golden rule; those who have the gold make the rules. You don't upset people with money, and you certainly don't tell them what to do with it, because—and here is the word—it is "theirs." They deserved it; it came to them by some special right of their effort or their personal value. You may ask the rich for some of their money, but never suppose you can make demands.

When it comes to the *practical* matters of how to manage money, *spiritual* leaders are out of their depth. So, let *practical* people deal with *practical* matters, and *spiritual* leaders deal with *spiritual* matters. Right? Not according to scripture.

Yet, some would say, "I wouldn't trust my pastor to be a part of my financial decision-making." And, I would say, "Then, you need a new pastor." I am amazed at how willing people are to submit their church to the leadership of a pastor that they would not trust to lead their family or business (due to character and integrity issues).

So, how about you? Would you be willing to sit down with a small group of Christian people to help you set a "personal" budget, a "business" budget, and a "ministry" budget? Assuming you found people of spiritual maturity and integrity, would you resent or appreciate the claims they might make on "your" assets on behalf of the Body of Christ?

The Root Causes of Greed

THE EMOTIONAL ROOT OF GREED IS IN THE TRUST WE PLACE IN OUR ASSETS.

I have a retirement account that the churches I served contributed to from the time I was twenty until I was thirty-four. The actual contributions were not large, but through "the miracle of compound interest" the total has become significant. Sometimes, it actually calms me to call the automated teller to get an update on the account balance. Lately, the account total has suffered, along with the stock market. Even though this is money I don't directly manage and can't access until retirement, I still get calmed or upset depending upon the activity of the account. I believe my feelings are the direct result of greed. I know that God has a plan for my future, and it is His responsibility to bring it about (with or without my retirement account).

That account is not to be trusted in. Whether it grows or declines has no real bearing on what God has in mind for me. My future is not secured or endangered by that account. The same is true for you. Your job, the equity in your house, your savings, your inheritance, and your retirement are not to be trusted in. God is not "taking them into account" in determining what He plans for your future. He will provide for His own purposes!

THE RELATIONAL ROOT OF GREED IS IN ATTRIBUTING VIRTUE
TO THOSE WITH ASSETS.

It has been true since the days of Job; we assume that if you have money it is because God has blessed you, because you are a good person. And if you are not a good person, then at least you are intelligent or at least you've got a wonderful personality or at least… there has got to be something good about you because you've got money.

I counseled with one "gentleman of means" who could not embrace the idea that he was more responsible for creating and maintaining the difficulties in his marriage than his wife was. I sensed that he wanted to believe me, but every time he asked anyone else about any given circumstance in his marriage, they agreed that his wife was more to blame. It is true that this husband was very self-assured and a persuasive communicator, but there was another dynamic that insulated him from being able to see his faults. Everyone he spoke to was dependent on him financially. Even his grown children all worked for him. He was not used to hearing anything negative about himself. And, when he did, it was too easy to explain away as envy or some other failure on his critic's part. (After all, they couldn't imagine the pressures and demands he lived with.)

Still, I think I would have been able to help him if he just hadn't had so much money.

He could not escape the idea that his financial success indicated some deep, abiding wisdom or virtue on his own part. He had trusted his instincts in making the difficult decisions that led to the creation of his fortune. He just couldn't set those instincts aside when they had been so beneficial to him.

THE SPIRITUAL ROOT OF GREED IS IN BELIEVING THAT ASSETS ARE SPIRITUALLY NEUTRAL.

Richard Foster says in *The Challenge of the Disciplined Life*:
What all this talk about stewardship fails to see is that money is not just a neutral medium of exchange but a "power" with a life of its own. And very often it is a "power" that is demonic in character. As long as we think of money in impersonal terms alone, no moral problems exist aside from the proper use of it. But when we begin to take seriously the biblical perspective that money is animated and energized by "powers," then our relationship to money is filled with moral consequence.

Accordingly, do you believe your life would be blessed if you won the next ten-million-dollar *Reader's Digest* sweepstakes? Would having money make you spiritually, emotionally, or relationally freer? The honest answer is "No." Only greed tells you otherwise. But, since our culture is so immersed in greed, we find it hard to even think in different terms.

The Cure for Greed: Sacrifice

Do you remember Zacchaeus, the "wee little man" who climbed the tree to see Jesus? He was a tax collector, and he had defrauded people. Jesus called him down out of the tree and invited Himself to dinner, which, in that culture, instituted intimate friendship. After dinner with Jesus, Zacchaeus pledged to give away half of his assets and to repay what he had stolen four times over.

And, Jesus proclaimed, "Today salvation has come to this house" (Lk 19:9). Zacchaeus had been delivered from the power of his assets; he had been delivered from his greed. That was the same nature of salvation that evaded the rich young ruler when Jesus confronted him and said, "Go, sell everything you have and give to the poor, and you will have treasure in heaven. Then come, follow me" (Mk 10:21).

All too often in American Christianity, "salvation" is considered a "conversion" to an agreement to follow Jesus based on an agreement that lifestyle changes will be discussed at a later date. For Jesus, the message was "Repent, for the kingdom of heaven is near" (Mt 4:17). Jesus confronted people's sin motivations, and if they repented of them He proclaimed His salvation. Jesus allowed His disciples to count the cost before choosing whether or not to follow Him. When Jesus presented the cost it almost always included losing social acceptance and financial control. I believe those are the two things that Jesus was talking about when He said to count the cost. Social acceptance was sacrificed at your baptism. Baptism represented more than a change in religion; it represented a change in cultural identity. It was like saying, "I am a baby and I'm starting over new, and I need a whole fresh beginning." It took a true brokenness for a person in that culture to allow himself to be baptized. And, you were baptized *into* the community of faith—covenant community. Here are the two primary obstacles to your being able to receive discipleship: social acceptance and financial control. Give these things up so that you can be saved. Count the cost, and enter into salvation.

Emotional Investment in the Lives of Those in Need

The cure for greed includes becoming emotionally invested in those whose needs can be met in our willingness to sacrifice our wants. Now understand, this is not sending your money to Washington, where it runs through three or four layers of bureaucracy before it comes back to help somebody. This is going directly to your neighbor, hand to hand, face to face, life to life, and becoming emotionally invested in this person. It means that when we send money to African missions, for instance, we are not doing it to alleviate guilt, look good, or feel good, but because we have allowed ourselves to develop a genuine love and concern for the African people and their needs. Unless you have made an emotional and personal connection with another person, even if it is just through pictures and prayer, you can't truly be generous to them. At the heart of generosity is a caring, life-to-life involvement with another person.

Once you make such a connection, you will realize that there is no way you will ever have enough or give enough to meet all needs. You will want to make every effort to free up the assets you do have in order to minister to others.

For instance, if somebody were to walk in today and give Plumbline Ministries five million dollars, we could continue our ministry indefinitely by investing it and living off the interest. But, we wouldn't. The need is too great. Our vision isn't about preserving or maintaining this ministry, it is about meeting the needs of people. And, since the needs are overwhelming, we would expand the ministry; hire on new counselors, expand our facilities, buy some ministry houses, increase our publications, etc. Soon we would have all that money obligated, and we would need more money, because we wouldn't have met all the needs that God has called us to meet. It would be gone, and we would be looking for more. Once you involve yourself, emotionally invest yourself in the needs of others, you will never have enough money to feel secure. (Note: I know that many ministries have established "foundations" to guarantee the long-term viability of the ministry. I can see the wisdom in that. I also see, and have experienced, the way such financial management cripples the passion and limits the vision of those called to the ministry. I have found overwhelming greed practiced consistently in the leadership of some wonderful outreach ministries.)

Once you embrace a vision (calling, gifting, and passion), you can never again afford to be greedy. Greed is always at the expense of a vision, for generosity considers it a great privilege to be able to invest in the lives of others. And when you do so, you will be open to consider whether you are keeping too much for yourself. Then simplicity of life becomes an attractive option for us. We will try to structure our lives to where it needs the minimum amount of our time and our energy and our money so that we have more to invest in others. It is not a sacrifice to live in a smaller house or drive an older car once you are captured by a vision. It is a means of doing what we want to do, which is to invest in the lives of others. Generosity is freedom to embrace vision and passion, to invest in others, and to experience covenant community.

Small Group Discussion

1) On a scale of one to ten (with one being very generous and ten being very greedy) rate yourself. State why.

2) Do you really believe that money is a "power"? If so, how?

3) Who is the most generous person you know? What makes you think so?

4) Pray for each other's struggle against greed.

Chapter Eight

Gluttony

"Therefore I endure everything for the sake of the elect, that they too may obtain the salvation that is in Christ Jesus, with eternal glory. Here is a trustworthy saying: If we died with him, we will also live with him; if we endure, we will also reign with him. If we disown him, he will also disown us; if we are faithless, he will remain faithful, for he cannot disown himself."

2 TIMOTHY 2:10–13

The definition of gluttony: Pampering yourself until it hurts in an effort to soothe a real or perceived neglect or abuse upon you.

In the scripture verse above, Paul is saying that we should expect to have three types of challenges in life:

1) sin motivations we need to die to,
2) circumstances we need to endure, and
3) consequences of following Jesus that we need to embrace.

We could also label these three categories as 1) temptations, 2) tribulations, and 3) trials. (It will also be helpful for you to note that they correspond respectively to the categories of 1) spiritual, 2) emotional, and 3) relational.) These are the three areas of our lives in which we can encounter pain and suffering. If we are unable to relate in a healthy way to these areas of our lives, they will become the motivation for gluttony within us.

This sin motivation is commonly associated with compulsions and addictions; whether it is workaholism, sexaholism, alcoholism, praiseaholism, anorexia, co-dependence, people-pleasing, or even running marathons or memorizing scripture. Anything we do in excess (to the point it actually is harmful to us) is motivated by a strong urge to "cover over" unwanted feelings. Usually, the more devastating the effects of our excesses, the stronger the feeling we are trying to cover over or avoid. The thing(s) we do in excess serve as a Band-Aid for our emotional, relational or spiritual wounds.

Manifestations of Gluttony

The first manifestation of gluttony is the inability to distinguish between temptations, tribulations, trials, and actual wounds. The three Ts (temptations, tribulations, and trials) are not attacks upon us as individuals and do not represent actual neglect or abuse toward us. They are natural parts of the lives of every disciple of Christ.

Far too many Christians have known true neglect and abuse. They may have been raised in a "sick" family, victimized by someone they trusted, or attacked randomly. They may have participated in a war, a cult, a gang, or an unhealthy marriage. Such neglect or abuse carries deep emotional, relational, and spiritual wounds that must be understood and processed before they can be healed. If these wounds are left unhealed, we will find Band-Aids to help soothe or hide the pain. Thus, gluttony can be a response to real neglect or abuse. However, gluttony is often the result of perceived neglect or abuse, when we believe we have been victimized by one or more of the three Ts.

In our pampered and indulged culture, it is all too easy for us to consider ourselves as "victims" anytime things are difficult for us. We can even accuse God of neglecting or abusing us if we don't have health, wealth, and success in all we attempt. However, the apostle Paul has instructed us to "die," "endure," and remain faithful in the face of the three Ts. So, let's look at each one individually.

Gluttony

Temptations

"If we died with him, we will also live with him" (2 Tm 2:11). This is in reference to a temptation, an invitation to sin. It's an invitation to please our carnal nature. When we resist our own carnal nature, the scripture refers to that as dying to self. When we resist temptation and we humble ourselves before God, it can literally feel like we are dying. "Died with him" is not just an analogy that Paul is using; it is a very descriptive term. Resisting temptation can feel like something is hurting and falling away inside of us, leaving a dull ache there.

Tribulations

"...[I]f we endure, we will also reign with him" (2 Tm 2:12a). Endure what? Well, a tribulation is a hardship of living in our fallen world. It is the negative aspects of living in a fallen world; ignorance, accidents, disease, corrupt governments, false religions, etc. When you lose your job due to a bad economy, are diagnosed with cancer, oversleep because your alarm failed, or your house is burglarized, you are facing a tribulation. It is unlikely that God is trying to teach you anything by your tribulations other than to "cast all your anxiety on him because he cares for you" (1 Pt 5:7).

During your tribulations, God is hurting for you and hurting with you. One of Jesus' strongest temptations was to strike a deal with the devil that would prevent you from having to endure the tribulations of this world (see Luke 4). As I understand it, the deal Satan offered was a trade of all authority over the nations (as things will be in the millennial reign following Jesus' return) for Jesus' acknowledgement and acceptance (worship) of him; Satan would be allowed to continue his scheming and tempting the hearts of men forever. Jesus was strongly tempted to save you and me from all our tribulations. Even today, Jesus would like to prevent all your temptations and rescue you from those you are currently experiencing.

The great wisdom and love God exercises in the fulfillment of His promises to us is beyond our understanding, but He asks us to trust Him (see 2 Corinthians 1:20). We all know God is able to work any miracle necessary to make our time on earth easier for us. Yet, His miracles are exercised according to His wisdom and love, not ours. Wisdom beyond ours may look like foolishness to us. And, love beyond ours may seem mean to us. Therefore, sometimes we may feel God is being foolish and mean to us and believe ourselves neglected or abused by Him. For instance, the death of a loved one, as painful and hurtful as that is, is not neglect or abuse. We can interpret it as such, can't we? We can say that God took that person from our lives. He wounded us. But no, that is not true. Death is a tribulation; it is a part of the nature of living within our fallen world, it is not something that God did to us.

Trials

"...[I]f we disown him, he will also disown us" (2 Tm 2:12b). A trial is an opportunity to deny or proclaim our faith among our peers. Trials are the stresses of life created by our ministry and peer relationships. Jesus made it clear to us that following him would have some negative consequences for us relationally (see John 15:18–27). These relational difficulties and stresses are trials to us. Even ministry, as we have defined it (intentionally entering into difficult situations with difficult people in hopes of affecting mutual spiritual growth), is a trial.

Sometimes, those we are reaching out to (or trying to minister alongside of) can neglect or abuse us. But, if someone were to reject us because of our faith, it would not mean that we had necessarily been abused. Trials are to be expected and embraced. If we resent them or take them personally, we are making ourselves susceptible to the sin motivation of gluttony.

> *"Consider it pure joy, my brothers, whenever you face trials of many kinds, because you know that the testing of your faith develops perseverance. Perseverance must finish its work so that you may be mature and complete, not lacking anything. If any of you lacks wisdom, he should ask God, who gives generously to all without finding fault, and it will be given to him."*

> JAMES 1:2–5

God's discipline is never abuse. I believe that the discipline God exercises in our life most often is to allow us to suffer the consequences of our sin. Since God shows us so much mercy and grace, we rarely experience the consequences of our sin. When God withholds His mercy and grace, we tend to think He is punishing us. He is not. He is disciplining us, because He loves us. He is not being vindictive or cruel. We are not being neglected or abused. If we are able to embrace His discipline, we will grow because of it. If not, we will feel abused, and, again, make ourselves susceptible to gluttony.

It is also important to note that the three Ts are not God's means of disciplining us. If you are unable to separate these aspects of your life in Christ, every time you experience anything negative you will tend to ask the question, "What is God trying to teach me?"

The Opposite of Gluttony is Wisdom

"If any of you lacks wisdom, he should ask God, who gives generously to all without finding fault, and it will be given to him" (Jas 1:5). Wisdom should not be confused with a word of knowledge or with hearing the specific will of God. Wisdom will not tell you what God's specific will is for any circumstance in your life. Wisdom will give us insight into God's nature. Wisdom will open our eyes to God's concern for and care of us.

The verse from James, quoted above, is followed by references to the three Ts. If we are not double-minded (doubting God's love for us and care of us), we will become strong in the face of the three Ts. If we do not doubt God, then the nature of our temptations, trials, and tribulations will become clear to us. We will understand how to respond to the circumstances of our lives. We will not falsely believe that we have been neglected or abused by God.

Real Neglect or Abuse

When those God intended to be closest to us (our parents, our churches, our spouses) neglect or abuse us, we are deeply wounded. When those who should be adding healthy and valuable input in our lives instead bring dysfunction and harm into them, we are doubly hurt. First, we are hurt by the absence of the good things God intended them to bring to us. Second, we are injured by the negative things they bring instead. As a Christian counselor, I am sometimes amazed that people so deeply wounded can still have the courage to look for healthy relationships or trust me (or anyone) to truly care for them. I'm reminded of one young lady who had been sexually molested by her father for twelve years (she finally moved away for college). She told me about going to get a massage by a sports therapist. When he began touching her inappropriately, she froze and could not speak. When she offered no resistance, he slowly escalated the sexual nature of the encounter. She remained still and quiet until he was finished. As soon as he left, she broke down, crying hysterically. She had been so effectively trained to submit to abuse by her father that she felt like she had no right to refuse anyone who insisted upon the use of her body.

This young lady's gluttony was evidenced in her perfectionism. She had to make straight As, keep her dorm room immaculate, keep her weight within 3 pounds of her norm, and keep her car serviced at all times. These Band-Aids didn't adequately cover her wounds, so she pushed herself harder. Eventually, she had a nervous breakdown. That's when we began counseling. Several months later she dropped out of counseling when I began directing her toward cutting off all ties with her father. Instead of facing the legitimate suffering this decision would cause, she chose to quit counseling. In the letter I received from her announcing her withdrawal from counseling, she thanked me for helping her get over some of her perfectionism and mentioned that her new boyfriend didn't like the idea of having a girlfriend that was in counseling. In other words, she had found a new Band-Aid. She would practice her gluttony relationally rather than pragmatically.

Our wounding can come from an alcoholic parent, a manipulative church leader, a self-serving schoolteacher, a trusted family member, or even from our government. However it comes, God has already stated His perspective: "And whoever welcomes a little child like this in my name welcomes me. But if anyone causes one of these little ones who believe in me to sin, it would be better for him to have a large millstone hung around his neck and to be drowned in the depths of the sea" (Mt 18:5–6).

Gluttony

The beginning point of gluttony is an inability to discern the difference between temptations, trials, tribulations, discipline, and wounding. We need to be able to respond to the three Ts and discipline as such. To interpret these aspects of our life as neglect or abuse is to believe a lie Satan tells us to nurture the sin motivation of gluttony.

Developing a Sense of Victimization

Feelings of victimization include helplessness, hopelessness, numbness, and inappropriate guilt and shame. Each of these feelings can be understood and processed by a survivor of neglect and abuse.

If you really were neglected or abused, you know that often the feeling of helplessness was all too real. A child has no means of self-protection. Perpetrators want the child to feel hopeless in order to facilitate continued abuse. Perpetrators are usually glad for their victims to become numb and detached, freeing them from expectations of fulfilling their God-intended role in their victim's life. And, possibly worst of all, perpetrators are skilled at making the child feel guilty for "causing" or "enjoying" the abuse.

However, as an adult, you can get help. You are not helpless. God is for you. Find a safe place, among safe people, to get the help you need. I know that the thought of even remembering all that you have been through makes you anxious, but there really is a healing process available to you. It is not hopeless. Don't let inappropriate guilt and shame stop you from getting the help you need. You can find surrogate parents, siblings, grandparents, etc. to take up the roles your perpetrator perverted. You can't do it alone, get over it, or just live with it. Your wounds cannot be covered with Band-Aids. The healing process is difficult, but you won't be alone in it.

If you misinterpreted the three Ts and discipline as neglect or abuse, it is time for you to put aside your double-mindedness (believing that God hasn't always acted in wisdom and love toward you), call upon Him for wisdom, and repent of your gluttony. Your perception of yourself as helpless and hopeless has been self-serving, justifying your gluttony. It is time for you to take responsibility for yourself. You must begin the difficult process of laying a firm foundation to build your life upon. You will need strict accountability for your time, energy, and money. You will need to disassociate yourself from friends who have facilitated your gluttony. You will need to seek out God's plan for your life and pursue it with a passion. Leave out any one of these directives, and your sin motivation will not be sufficiently safeguarded against. You will continue to act out self-destructively.

Identifying Means of Escaping Your Feelings

Recovering addicts have learned to identify their "drug of choice." It is an appropriate term, recognizing the job of the "drug" is to mask the pain of our wounds (real or perceived). The "drug" may be alcohol, pills, or weed. It may be a job, gambling, sex, exercise, friends, church activities, television, eating, talking, perfectionism, money, activities, hobbies, or even our children. Anything that masks, replaces, or crowds out our unwanted feelings could be our drug of choice.

Sometimes, the drug is socially acceptable or even encouraged. Working in excess of God's plan for your life is easy to justify, ignore, or even misidentify as a virtue (diligence). Exercising in excess and over-investing ourselves in our children are often thought of in very positive terms. But, you must be willing to be self-reflective, asking yourself if your motivation is to provide yourself with a drug.

Pampering Yourself Until It Hurts

The glutton must take enough of his drug to cover his true wounds. Therefore, the amount of drug he needs to take to accomplish its purpose will always be hurtful to him. For instance, if the glutton's drug of choice is food, he will not be satisfied with eating a small amount, no matter how good it tastes. Until his belly is stretched beyond what is comfortable, it has yet to create a feeling that covers over the wound. The drug must create an alternative feeling for the wounded person to focus on. If the feeling is not very strong, or quickly goes away, it will not serve as an appropriate Band-Aid. So, the glutton must take in a sufficient amount of his drug of choice to create feelings strong enough to cover the feelings seeping from the wound. Such an amount of any drug will ultimately be harmful to the glutton.

Gluttony

The Root Causes of Gluttony

THE EMOTIONAL ROOT OF GLUTTONY IS DENIAL.

You are probably familiar with the role that denial plays in the life of a glutton. Denial can be the most difficult aspect of gluttony to break through. Denial protects us from recognizing both the cause and the effects of our gluttony.

Denial may be directed toward the wound (the cause). I have had a good and godly man tell me that he "refuses to live life as a victim." He didn't mean that he was committed to exploring the consequences of his victimization and developing healthy ways of processing and healing his wounds. He was telling me that he was committed to pretending that nothing significant really happened and that there are no lasting effects upon him. I have tried to break through his denial by using a phrase that has become almost a cliché for me: "you don't get to choose whether you will be a victim or not. The choice was taken from you; that is the very nature of victimization."

Or, denial may be directed toward minimizing the destructive nature of the gluttony (the effects). I'm told by gluttons that their drinking (or drug of choice) isn't hurting anyone, is none of my business, and shouldn't be judged.

Denial can be strong, because there is something within me that knows that if you take away my Band-Aid, I'm going to bleed all over everything. Something within me says, "Don't you dare try and take away my Band-Aid! I'm scared to death of what I might find behind it."

THE RELATIONAL ROOT OF GLUTTONY IS ENABLING.

Denial is such a strong coping mechanism that it draws others to aid in maintaining and protecting it. Whole families can adopt roles based upon facilitating an individual's gluttony. Finding or training others to enable our gluttony is the relational root of this sin motivation. Gluttons have to find counterparts who will accommodate having the drug of choice around and to deal with the consequences. Sometimes the enabler accommodates the consequences of the gluttony based on an inappropriate definition of love, submission, loyalty, acceptance, etc. Sometimes the enabler is motivated by her own gluttonous need for acceptance, approval, or love. And, sometimes the enabler is a child who doesn't really have any other option (this is how the sin motivation gets passed from one generation to the next).

THE SPIRITUAL ROOT OF GLUTTONY IS WHEN WE ATTACK THE CHARACTER OF GOD BY SOMETIMES BELIEVING; 1) GOD DOESN'T REALLY CARE THAT WE WERE NEGLECTED AND/OR ABUSED, 2) GOD HIMSELF HAS BEEN NEGLECTFUL AND/OR ABUSIVE TOWARD US.

Sometimes it was members or leaders within the church that were the perpetrators. It then becomes very difficult for the victim to not entertain accusations against God. It is no easier for someone abused by a parent to believe that God loves and cares for them (after all, God chose their parents for them). Although there are theological explanations for why God allows such tragedies to continue, none can answer every question and accusation. Yet, there is an ultimate proof of God's love for you. The ultimate proof that God cares for those victimized by those who should have loved them is that God allowed His only son to also be victimized by those who should have loved Him. The crucifixion of Jesus is God's effort to erase every doubt and accusation against His love for us. We can still entertain such thoughts, but they are nonsense in light of the torture and death of Jesus.

The Cure for Gluttony: Gain Wisdom

Gain understanding of yourself, your world, and your God. Join a twelve-step group. "Work the steps, and the steps will work for you."

We do not have to re-invent the wheel. The emotional, relational, and spiritual roots of gluttony are addressed in the twelve steps. The group I have participated in and refer my counselees to is called Celebrate Recovery. They offer Christ-centered recovery programs to "those with habits, hurts, and hang-ups." Hey, that sounds like you. You have some habits, hurts, and hang-ups. I know it sounds like me.

Twelve-step programs offer their participants encouragement in addressing their dysfunctional thinking toward themselves, others, and the world. Biblically based twelve-step programs also help address the participant's relationship with God. In addition to ministry to the addict (glutton) they usually offer ministry to those who have enabled and/or suffered the consequences of the gluttony.

One of the healthiest dynamics of the twelve-step programs is that they confront the power of shame. Participants introduce themselves as struggling, striving, growing Christians. The way I introduced myself to the group the last time I attended was: "I'm Terry, a grateful believer in Jesus Christ, celebrating recovery from attachment disorders and currently struggling with sloth." Everyone introduced themselves in a similar manner.

Oh, what a powerfully healing dynamic it would be if we actually introduced ourselves to each other in church this way! Why don't we? Some might say, "We don't introduce ourselves in church this way because not everyone is struggling with sin they way you (Terry) do." I have to tell you, I simply do not believe this. Moreover, I think that thought is thoroughly unbiblical.

Some might say, "We don't want to expose our innocent children to our personal struggles," or "We need to present the message that God is stronger than our sin nature," or "Our struggles are very personal and should be kept private." What would you say?

I'll tell you why I might not be willing to practice the dynamic of confessing my struggles in church. I don't know if it is safe.

Actually, I've found a place to worship where I feel safe. I look forward to opportunities to share my current struggles. I know what a blessing it is to not have to be anxious about what others might be thinking of me. And, I want that for you! Hopefully this book can be used to help shape your church into a safe place for you.

Small Group Discussion

1) On a scale of one to ten (with one being very wise and ten being very gluttonous) rate yourself. State why.

2) If you struggle with gluttony, have you determined if your wounding is real or perceived? If your wounding is real, what steps have you taken to gain freedom from the wounding?

3) Who is the wisest person you know? What makes you think so?

4) Pray for each other's struggle against gluttony.

Chapter Nine

Envy

Now Abel kept flocks, and Cain worked the soil. In the course of time Cain brought some of the fruits of the soil as an offering to the Lord. But Abel brought fat portions from some of the firstborn of his flock. The Lord looked with favor on Abel and his offering, but on Cain and his offering he did not look with favor. So Cain was very angry, and his face was downcast. Then the Lord said to Cain, "Why are you angry? Why is your face downcast? If you do what is right, will you not be accepted? But if you do not do what is right, sin is crouching at the door; it desires to have you, but you must master it.".... And while they were in the field, Cain attacked his brother Abel and killed him. Then the Lord said to Cain, "Where is your brother Abel?" "I don't know," he replied. "Am I my brother's keeper?".... Cain said to the Lord, "My punishment is more than I can bear. Today you are driving me from the land, and I will be hidden from your presence; I will be a restless wanderer on the earth, and whoever finds me will kill me."

GENESIS 4:1–14

The definition of envy; a negative critique of God's plan for your life due to comparisons with others and/or expectations of your own. There are two forms of envy: comparison-based and expectation-based. Cain's envy was comparison-based. Cain's anger toward Abel was based upon the fact that God had accepted Abel's offering, but not his own. Cain's sin manifestation was anger. His sin motivation was envy. The truth is that Cain's anger toward Abel had nothing to do with Abel.

For some reason, Cain's offering was unacceptable to God. Although there are several explanations offered by theologians as to why this would be, the author of Genesis does not tell us exactly why God rejected Cain's offering. Maybe it was because God saw the envy in Cain's heart and used the setting of worship to confront Cain with it. I can attest that God has often convicted me of my sin motivations during times of worship.

However, Cain was not willing to see his sin motivation. Even after God pointed out that Cain's anger was really an acceptance issue, Cain continued to nurse his anger. Notice that God assured Cain that he could overcome his sin motivation (anger) if he would acknowledge his sin motivation (envy). God was willing to offer Cain the acceptance he craved if he would stop comparing himself to his brother.

Cain committed the first murder, and his punishment does not seem just. It is not an example of what our legal systems should do with murderers. It was a punishment meant to give Cain an opportunity to face his envy. Cain was stripped of everything he could use to compare his life to others: his possessions, his place in the family, and his personal power. He lost his land, his home, and was scared for his life. All that he had going for him was "a mark" of God's acceptance. Yes, God still offered His acceptance to Cain. Cain had compared God's acceptance of him to God's acceptance of Abel and had envied Abel. Now, God's acceptance was the only thing Cain had left. Did Cain receive God's acceptance? We don't know. We know that Cain's envy was strong enough to move him to murder. Even when everything else was stripped from him, Cain may have not valued God's acceptance. He may have insisted that God accept him on his own terms. God had already rejected his grain offering, so I can't think that God would accommodate Cain's expectations. Cain would be judged for his envy, unless during the course of his discipline he was able to lay it aside.

We generally think of envy in terms of comparing our lifestyles to someone else's and determining that life (God) has not been kind or fair to us. Sometimes our envy is based upon unmet expectations. And, again, we can decide that life has not been as fair or kind to us as we have a right to expect. However, at the heart of envy is an even deeper issue. At the heart of envy is a willingness to compare my value as a human being to another. Cain's interpretation of why his offering was rejected was wrong. We know that God did not compare Cain's offering to Abel's. Cain's interpretation was wrong. He was envious of Abel for no good reason. His anger toward Abel was totally misplaced. Cain's sin motivation of envy manifested in anger toward Abel (jealousy).

It is important that you see the process of sin: It began within Cain as envy; it led to a wrong interpretation by Cain (jealousy); it manifested as anger toward Abel.

Envy, like all sin motivations, is subtle. It is a matter of our thinking, interpretations, and expectations that we may not even be aware of. When an envious person is asked what they are feeling, they will usually tell you that they are angry or depressed. They don't usually say, "I'm so terribly envious of what I expect my life to be that I'm becoming clinically depressed" or "I'm so overwrought with envy toward someone that it makes me feel better to hate them," but bitterness and depression are the two most frequent manifestations of envy.

When we are "moody," it may be because we are tired or mildly sick, or it may be because we are harboring envy. We may be irritable, defensive, unmotivated, critical, demanding, grumpy, listless, distracted, emotional, or withdrawn when we are harboring envy.

We may also begin manifesting sloth or gluttony when motivated by envy. Envy is a form of self-victimization in which we interpret that something hurtful and harmful has happened to us, based upon comparing our lives to those of others or our own expectations.

Envy Based on Comparisons

Sometimes we talk about "keeping up with the Joneses." Now I want to make an issue of that word "up" because I have a question: "Which way is up?" If the Joneses have more possessions or they get to do more things, does that mean that they are "up"?

There is no sin in acknowledging that others may have opportunity to do some things or to have some things that we don't have. But, when we think that such opportunities indicate that others have been given better, more fulfilling life plans and purposes than ourselves, we are practicing envy.

Our culture is a free-market society, driven by a company's ability to produce, distribute, advertise, and sell a product or service. Advertising is intended to accomplish a purpose: to promote envy. Advertisements are developed to send two messages: 1) Your life is incomplete without our product or service, and 2) our company's product or service is best (based upon price, style, performance, or sex appeal). In this chapter we are concerned with that first message. The commercials are developed to convince us that our lives might really be incomplete and unfulfilling if we miss out on the offered product or service. And, unless we are very intentional about combating this brainwashing, we will begin to absorb that message. We will find ourselves looking "up" to what advertisements say we need.

This message is not just promoted by advertisers, but is a presupposition of our culture espoused on every front. It is the message of "missing out" if you didn't attend certain events, or can't perform at a certain levels, or haven't experienced certain things. The message is subtle but adamant; God's plan for your life is not good enough!

Envy Based on Expectations

Anyone can readily recognize the disastrous potential of unrealistic expectations for a person's life. Yet, even our churches seem to promote to picture of the holy man to whom faith and righteousness come easy. Hopefully, you have been delivered from that heresy through your previous study of *Stickman Theology*. But, alongside the holy man ("Captain Glorious"), other false images have been offered as models of unrealistic expectations; the "self-made man," the "superwoman," the "always focused family man," the "model citizen," and the always attractive "well-rounded" intellectual-athletic-romantic-mechanical person, among others. Beware unrealistic expectations. Even as we laugh at them they can be nagging at our souls.

However, envy is by no means limited to unrealistic expectations. Any expectation, even highly possible ones, can be envy's fodder. Once any expectation becomes attached to the notion that our life would be unfulfilled if we were to lack it, we are practicing envy. For instance, I am blessed to have a wonderful wife, yet if God had made it clear to me that it was his specific will for me to never marry I have to believe that my life would have been just as blessed, if only in different ways. Another example: I love learning and flourish in academic settings, therefore I could envy the opportunity to complete a doctorate or Ph.D. program and teach in a seminary. However, to date, my life has been full and complete in other ways. You see, the best plans we could make for ourselves (reasonable or not) cannot compete with what God is doing in our lives today. To think otherwise is envy.

Even biblical expectations of others can be the source of envy. The wife, married for fourteen years to a lukewarm Christian, who is still angry that he is not the "spiritual leader of the family," is being envious. Living in bitterness toward someone who fails to meet your expectation of them is envy, even if the expectation is biblical. This wife should accept her husband's choice and find other godly means for spiritual expression, fulfillment, and intimacy. God's plan and purpose for her life is not being thwarted by her husband's failure any more than God's plan for Joseph was thwarted by his brothers selling him into slavery, or Potivar's wife having him imprisoned falsely. Although others can offend and hurt you, only you can prevent the plan and purpose of God from being fulfilled in your life.

Other Manifestations of Envy

Envy raises the question, "Why does the other guy have it better than me?"

Envy encourages us to compare ourselves to "the other guy." If we decide that "we have it better" than someone else, it is easy for us to credit ourselves with some reason why: We work harder, have better character, have more common sense, aren't weird, have more or better faith, understand people better, are more sincere, are more honest with ourselves, etc. Pride is always ready to answer the question of why things are going better for us than for the other guy. But, what do we tell ourselves when we compare our lives with the other guy's and he "has it better than us"? Then, envy can begin to work its way into our thinking.

In combating the influence of envy in those for whom it has become a stronghold, I have discovered two thoughts that must be exposed, countered, and defeated. The first thought is exposed in how we answer the envious question of whether or not the person who has it better than us is somehow better than us.

Please take a moment to reflect on this question, "If someone has it better than me, does that mean that they are somehow better than me?"

Now, let's answer the question. The answer is yes; the other guy is somehow better than you. We are all created equal in value to God, but we have different attributes, different skills, different personality types; we are different. And there are some things other people can do better than we can. As a matter of fact, there is no one you know who is not better than you in some ways. We can be envious of that and think we have to be just as good, or we can embrace each other for that very same reason, that the other person has something to offer and we can respect and value each other.

Among Christians, envy will often point to those who practice unrighteousness and raise the question of why they have it better than you. The healthy, biblical answer is, "The advantage you see in their lives over yours may very well be due to the fact that they are better than you in some way." Furthermore, God asks you to be glad for them and to be drawn to love them better because you see something wonderful that God has created in them. It is envy that keeps a Christian from loving the sinner. It is envy that makes us resent the kindnesses and blessings God brings into their lives.

A second question raised by envy is, "Does God has different rules for me than for others?" When we compare our lives with others, envy encourages us to recognize that others seem to be able to get away with things that God would quickly discipline us for. Even fellow Christians seem to have more freedoms than we believe God would allow us. Does this mean that God has different rules for different people?

Again, I would ask you to formulate an answer to this question in your mind before reading further. Does God have different rules for different people? Yes, He does. Please, don't misunderstand this point. This is not a surrender to the philosophy of situational ethics or a denial of moral and ethical absolutes. It is an acknowledgement of different personalities, cultures, and perspectives. Racism, for instance, is grounded in envy that won't accept that differences in cultures are totally inconsequential in determining the worth of any individual. So, yes, God may have some different rules for the white person and the black person (but not always). God may have some different rules for the poor person and the rich person. God may have some different rules for the preacher's kid and the atheist's kid. It may be God's will for one to social drink and the other not. One may vote Republican while the other votes Democrat and both be following God's will for them (can you believe it?).

What were the rules concerning Cain's offering? We don't know. We do know God's purpose for the offering: an expression of obedience, sacrifice, praise, and worship. God's purposes for us are the same: to inspire and impart faith, hope, and love. His rules to those ends may vary according to any number of things, including our race, intellect, personalities, education, form of government, time in history, social standing, or level of material wealth. Envy, however, will inspire us to racism and bigotry of all sorts. Envy inspires a judgmentalism that keeps us from seeing each other's hearts, because we won't believe that God could have some different rules for us than for others.

Embracing Alternatives to Envy

So, Cain's offering was rejected while Abel's was accepted. What was Cain supposed to do about it?

He could be receptive to God's purposes in him, or he could ask for fairness. We are back to this issue that is so strong in America today, this concept of fairness. He could have been receptive and said, "Okay, Lord. Sin is knocking at the door. You have rebuked me. Now, let's go to work on this." Instead, he hardened his heart and complained, not just against his brother but against God.

Cain had the option of comparing himself with his brother and hating him or focusing on God's work in his own life. God is asking us to trust His plan and purpose for our lives. Comparing our lives with others is a clear indication that we have lost focus on God's plans and purposes in our own lives.

Finally, as envy's work progresses within us, we have the choice to "get even" (whatever that means) with others or embrace God's call upon our lives. Cain's envy was manifested in his anger. He murdered his brother. God offered him the alternative of embracing His plan and purpose when He asked, "Cain, where is your brother Abel? Cain said, "Well, am I my brother's keeper?" And the answer, of course, is, "Yes; yes, you are."

The alternative to envy is contentment with God's plans and purposes. We can be receptive to God's plans and purposes, or we can grasp after our notions of fairness. We can obsessively compare and compete with others, or we can set our focus on God's work in our lives. We can invent ways to get even with others, or we can embrace God's callings on our lives. One alternative feeds envy; the other nourishes a soul of contentment.

The Root Causes of Envy

The roots of envy are fear of losing, and grasping after, and trying to create our own 1) sense of life purpose, 2) personal power, and 3) access to the presence of God.

So the roots of envy are fear of loss of purpose, power, and access to the presence of God. That is exactly what the result of envy was for Cain. He lost his sense of purpose in that he was driven from the land. He lost the presence of God, saying, "I will be hidden from your presence." And, he lost his sense of personal power, so he said, "I will be running for my life. People will be trying to kill me. I have no power."

God asks us to trust Him to provide life purpose, power, and His presence as He sees fit, not according to our expectations (no matter how biblical you may think your expectations are).

Let's look at each of these objects of envy separately:

1) LIFE PURPOSE: If you don't have a sense of God's purposes in your life, you need to re-read the chapter on sloth. However, if you do have a sense of God's purposes in your life, then you must know that they are uniquely your own and not to be compared with others. For instance,

being in full-time ministry is not a higher calling than being employed in any other manner. Being in a position to give money is not a higher calling than offering any other kindness. Being more highly educated is not a higher calling than any other responsible exercise of our intelligence. The value of your life purposes cannot be contrasted with Mother Teresa, Billy Graham, or the president of the United States. Those who cannot grasp this concept are in the grips of envy.

2) POWER: Power can be measured in terms of corporate hierarchy charts (who is the boss?), social and financial status, attractiveness, strength of personality, physical abilities, intellectual achievements, etc. And, the truth is that you have all the power God needs you to have!

As Christians we must be careful to always think of power in terms of influence, not control. If you feel the need to control others, even for their own good (children twelve and under excluded) you are practicing envy. God never intended for you to have control over others. The most prevalent example of envy I see is when husbands try to control their wives or wives try to control their husbands. They may even quote scripture in order to attempt to gain control; Ephesians 5 encourages husbands to sacrifice for their wives and wives to submit to their husbands. Anyone who has ever told their spouse that the Bible says they should submit to them or sacrifice for them has already distorted the scriptures and participated in envy. Scripture references to sacrifice and submission are encouraging the spouses to let go of their attempts to influence the other, not encouraging them to demand the right to exercise control. When submission is demanded (even by quoting scripture) what is expected is subjugation (not submission). The same is true when sacrifices are demanded. Husbands and wives can only offer sacrifice and submission when they are offered as gifts with no obligation claimed.

There are any number of books written on the biblical means of exercising power as influence (not control). *Boundaries* by Drs. Cloud and Townsend is a very popular and helpful course of study in the proper exercise of influence in relationships.

Those with financial, social, moral, physical, intellectual, or even spiritual power must be very aware of the temptations to exercise control over others. If they are not very sensitive to exercise their power only as influence, they will fall into control without intending to (but enjoying it nonetheless).

3) THE PRESENCE OF GOD: A truth that can easily be lost concerning our spiritual lives is that God's presence with us is assumed by faith. Sometimes we can "feel" His presence, "sense" His nearness, "hear" His voice, or otherwise be "moved" by Him. But no one has the right or the power to control or demand God's presence. We don't get to control how or if God makes His presence known to us. Nothing guarantees us a sense of God's presence, neither spiritual disciplines nor means of grace.

Still, there are those who try to evoke the presence of God instead of simply presenting themselves to God for Him to determine how and whether they will actually experience Him. There are those who seek after feelings of peace, joy, or assurance. There are those who pursue feelings associated with God's presence through worship, speaking in tongues, working of miracles, being slain in the Spirit, or gaining revelations or insights into His word. All of these are meant to be given as God determines, not at our insistence. Pursuing a sense of God's presence or approval is an act of envy.

THE EMOTIONAL ROOT OF ENVY IS A LOST SENSE OF PERSONAL PURPOSE.
When I really don't think that my purpose is as important as someone else's purpose, I have fallen prey to envy. Who would you say is the most important person working for God in your local church? I think that what we have to say is, "Me!" This is a paradox, because each individual should be saying the same thing: "Because of God's love of me, God's giftings and callings in me, I'm very important to God's purposes."

We must never say, "I am just...." Remember, "just" is the deplorable word.

THE RELATIONAL ROOT OF ENVY IS A LOST SENSE OF POWER.
We feel like we have to get up to where the influencers are. And the truth of the matter is the most powerful influencer could be the least on the

social ladder. That is exactly what Paul said was the nature of each of us when we were chosen by God. He says God didn't choose the wealthy or the intelligent or the powerful of this world, but He chose the weak in which to manifest His power. It is a paradox that turned the world upside down. So, do you know who the most influential person is? It is the person working in godliness; one who may not exercise any political, financial, or relational power but still has spiritual power.

THE SPIRITUAL ROOT OF ENVY IS A LOST SENSE OF GOD'S PRESENCE.
Now, understand when I say "sense of God's presence," I am not speaking of just the physical sense, where we feel the presence of God. There are going to be times when God doesn't allow His presence to be felt. Why? Well, simply because we walk by faith, not by sight. And sight is a sense. And if we are constantly seeking after sensing the presence of God, we are not walking by faith and rejoicing in the confidence of the presence of God, the promise of God, and embracing the reality of a worldview that says God is constantly at work in and around us. So we are not just talking about sensing or having a feeling of God's presence; it is having a conviction, a real worldview that we walk in that God is with us in this moment. Not with us twiddling His thumbs but with us, acting on our behalf, running ahead of us, even running behind, all about working very hard on our behalf.

The Cure for Envy: Contentment

The cure is the same as all the others, which is to take responsibility for these motivations, to identify what your motivation is and submit it to the work of God. I hope that you are well aware that none of the "cures" we have been presenting are those that we can grasp and make happen at our own choosing and in our own timing. Even our expectation of "curing our envy" can be envy.

We do not attempt to offer a course in overcoming envy (or any other of the Seven Deadly Sins). We do, however, want the reader to make an informed decision about trusting God for their sanctification. We want the reader to have an idea of what changes God will be working in us, what we are offering to give up, and what the alternative(s) to our sin may be. The alternative to envy is contentment.

Contentment requires an intentional and repeated battle against entertaining the comparison-based and expectation-based critiques of our life. Contentment is 1) a firm confidence that God has provided all that we need for abundant life, and 2) a growing trust that our part in the purposes of the kingdom are both specifically suited to us and eternally significant.

Let's look at each of these aspects of contentment individually:

1)   Contentment is a firm confidence that God has provided all that we need for abundant life. What is your definition of "abundant life"? I believe that abundant life is more life than you thought possible. It is more highs and more lows. It is more love and more hurt. It is more hopes and more disappointments. It is more vision and more frustration. It is more healing and growth, and it is more humility and struggle.

I have heard sermons and read books where abundant life was assumed to mean something like, "things get better and easier." When thought of in these terms the promise of abundant life will be a source of envy within us. The scripture never depicts a single Christian or Old Testament hero for whom things got better and easier as they matured in their faith.

Within our culture abundant life most likely is equated with a well-provided-for retirement. Once our biggest obligations are fulfilled (our careers, raising our children, etc.), then we are finally able to relax and enjoy ourselves. In other words, we can be convinced that abundant life means less life—less stress, fewer commitments, fewer challenging relationships, less need for healing, and certainly less need for growth. Can you see how this line of thinking strips away our contentment and empowers our envy?

2)   Contentment is a growing trust that our part in the purposes of the kingdom are both specifically suited to us and eternally significant. Contentment comes in knowing that God has given us an invitation to join Him in specific things that He is doing. (You may recognize this concept from the *Experiencing God* study by Henry Blackaby.) The work that God

is doing is His responsibility to accomplish, but we have been offered significant roles in some of those works. The roles we are offered are specifically designed to utilize our unique strengths, weaknesses, giftings, woundings, personalities, passions, needs, and even our unique (healthy) wants.

Contentment is a growing trust in God's willingness and ability to take all the people of the earth and all His eternally significant purposes and come up with roles that each of us fit so well. Often we only see through hindsight how He has actually accomplished these things. In the meantime, God asks us to trust Him.

The illustration is often given of how the backside of a needlework looks ragged and chaotic, but the front is a beautiful creation. Contentment comes from being able to trust God's purpose, power, intimate knowledge of us, and commitment to us even when our lives look like the backside of the needlework.

Small Group Discussion

1) On a scale of one to ten (with one being very content and ten being very envious) rate yourself. State why.

2) If you struggle with envy, are you inclined to comparison-based or expectation-based critiques of your life?

3) Who is the most content person you know? What makes you think so?

4) Pray for each other's struggle against envy.

Chapter Ten

Anger

"Dear brothers, take note of this: Everyone should be quick to listen, slow to speak, and slow to become angry, for man's anger does not bring about the righteous life that God desires."

JAMES 1:19–20

The sin of anger: an unwillingness or inability to work through negative situations in a productive manner.

This sin motivation will be difficult to discuss until we address one issue: We need to distinguish between the feeling of anger and the sin of anger.

The Feeling of Anger

The feeling of anger is not good or bad, right or wrong. Like our other feelings, anger serves an important purpose. The feeling of anger is an emotional motivator for seeking change. The feeling of anger is a motivator to hold those accountable for their inappropriate actions (or lack of appropriate actions). As Beverly Engel states in *Honor Your Anger*, "Anger is a necessary and important emotion. It signals that something is wrong in a relationship, in your environment, or in yourself." (Note: for a more thorough discussion of the feeling of anger see *Stickman Theology*, chapter 8.)

The Sin of Anger

The sin of anger can originate with two different dynamics: 1) When we are legitimately offended (someone has truly "done us wrong") and we react in a way that does not work through the situation appropriately, and 2) when we are not legitimately offended but react in anger to a negative situation as if we had been legitimately offended. These observations are detailed in *The Angry Christian* by Andrew Lester, who claims, "Scripture does not lobby for the eradication of anger, but is instead concerned about *why* we are angry and *how to express* anger ethically so that we don't behave destructively." We will examine each of these dynamics in depth in this chapter.

Denying or Suppressing Feelings of Anger

So, is it always wrong to feel angry? No, not at all. Anger is oftentimes an appropriate, godly response to sinful behavior. Sometimes it is very inappropriate and even sinful of us not to be angry. Anger is sin only when we don't respond to legitimate offenses in a productive manner.

The scriptures give accounts of times when Jesus was angry. Still, we have difficulty embracing appropriate anger. Maybe this is because it is easier for us to avoid or deny our feelings of anger than to work through them productively with those who offend us (notice that this motivation is still the sin of anger). Maybe we don't know how to work through some instances of anger productively (still sin). Maybe we are afraid that if we acknowledge our feelings of anger that we won't represent them appropriately (more sin). Maybe we are locked into a relationship in which an expression of anger (no matter how healthy) only makes things worse (if we are adults, this is still sin).

In one of the great ironies of our Christian culture, the anger-is-always-sin message is sometimes intentionally taught and often indirectly promoted in our churches. Christians mistake the messages of unity and forgiveness as an obligation to suppress or deny anger instead of embracing the difficult and sensitive work of processing anger is healthy ways. Therefore, the church becomes a promoter of the sin of anger ("an unwillingness or inability to work through negative situations in a productive manner").

We know that Jesus did not sin in His anger, that His anger was emotionally appropriate and that His responses were just. We have created terms like "righteously indignant" to distinguish what Jesus felt from what we may feel at times. I have even heard it taught that Jesus never was angry for His own sake, only for the sake of others. In other words, it was okay for Jesus to feel anger but not for us. I disagree! Denying our feelings of anger is still sin, because it does not allow us to work through it in a productive manner.

Recently, I was told by a colleague how terribly bad they thought something I had written was. Then my colleague asked me if I had "my feelings hurt." I felt like I was being challenged to not get mad. As if becoming offended by an attack on me was an indication of *my* spiritual immaturity. I responded to my colleague by saying, "Of course, how else is a person who was just attacked supposed to feel?" Then, together, we worked through the situation productively. (I like giving examples of when I did something right!)

MY ILLUSTRATION HAS TWO POINTS:

1) As previously mentioned, we sometimes think of ourselves as more mature if we deny or suppress our feelings of anger. I do believe that the more mature person is capable of "ducking" some offensive remarks. They do not deny their feeling of anger. Ducking or having thick skin may serve us well in helping us choose the time and means of working through an offense productively. However, these skills can become a coping mechanism that keeps us from ever working through a negative situation productively.

2) Although denying, minimizing, or dismissing my feelings of anger may have made that moment with my coworker easier, long-term our relationship would be worse. The feeling of anger serves a holy purpose of energizing us to address the negatives involved in any long-term relationship.

I gave one particularly anger-inhibited young woman the assignment of rewriting Jesus' confrontational words to the Pharisees recorded in Matthew 23:23-28. Her homework was to express the legitimate anger she feels toward her Christian friends who abandoned her during a time of need. This is what she came up with:

> Shame on you, you so-called friends! You are shallow fakes. You say you'll pray for me and go to Bible study with me, but you bail when things aren't pretty. You completely neglect the important parts of friendship—patience, unconditional love, and support. You should be providing all of these things as a friend. You talk about how good of a friend you are but you are not! You are like a person who bitches about an unreceived phone call but never picks up the damn phone. Shame on you, you so-called friends! You are shallow fakes. You work so hard to make yourselves look pretty, loving, and innocent but inside you are full of self-serving ways that don't allow you to care about anyone but yourself. So-called friends, you are being fooled! First, get over yourself and then maybe you can become truly pretty, loving, and innocent. Shame on you, you so-called friends! You are shallow fakes. You are like a sad imitation of a caring person. Outside, you seem to genuinely care, but inside, you freak as soon as anything breaks from "normalcy." That is what you are like. By "knowing" you, people think they can depend on you and trust you, but on the inside you have no tolerance for reality if it brings anything but sugarcoated attending to you and your sappy life.

Only after we identify the true depth of our anger can we offer forgiveness and practice healthy reconciliation.

I once counseled with a couple who had not kissed each other for over seven years. They would never have cussed at each other, screamed at each other, or threatened divorce. They considered such actions to be sinful, and exercised a strict control over themselves to prohibit these actions. Yet, I had to tell them that the cussers, yellers, and even those who threatened to divorce might be healthier and less sinful than them. They had been unwilling or unable to work through their offenses in a productive way. As a matter of fact, they had both given up on the possibility. In their bitterness and resentment, each considered the other to be "too sick" to deal with. And, by the time I saw them, I'm not at all sure that both of them weren't correct. Although they were both highly principled people who functioned well emotionally and relationally outside their marriage, within their marriage they had lived with their dysfunctions, resentments, and coping mechanisms for so long that they were unable to trust each other or risk themselves in healthy conflict resolution. They were locked in a stronghold of the sin of anger.

Healthy long-term relationships require that we face our conflicts honestly and diligently try to resolve them.

Even though my wife and I married too young and were not equipped with conflict resolution skills, we did try. Sometimes we tried in the wrong ways and our conflicts escalated, but we were trying. I knew she was trying, and she knew I was trying. Sometimes it seemed like that was all we had going for us. And (with the grace of God), it was enough!

I hope that you are more mature and have more relationship skills than we did. However, if you don't, don't give up. Find someone to help you. Don't surrender to anger!

Four Manifestations of Anger

If someone has actually acted inappropriately toward us (or failed to fulfill an obligation to us) we then have the opportunity to sin in anger or to respond to the feeling of anger in appropriate ways. There are a number of good books on appropriate conflict resolution; books on forgiveness, boundaries, decision-making, etc. We will only be able to touch on these skills (near the conclusion of this chapter).

Our goal in this section is to describe some ways that we inappropriately deal with offences:

1) AGGRESSIVENESS: This may be what most people think of when discussing the sin of anger. Aggressiveness can be illustrated as "fighting fire with fire." When someone is being negative toward us, the aggressive person will be equally negative back (or even escalate the level of negativity). Someone sends a ball of negativity toward me, and I lash out at it with my

own negativity to try and keep it away. Even though aggressiveness may make the situation better for the moment, it creates a multitude of wounds and walls in relationships.

Aggressive behavior can range from contemptuous neglect, to various forms of manipulation, to physical, emotional, or sexual abuse.

2) PASSIVENESS: Passive people are sometimes mistaken as patient people. Not so! Passiveness is still a refusal to work through the conflict productively. Passiveness may even encourage the offender to continue in his or her offenses because of lack of any negative consequences to them or because of an honest expectation that others shouldn't be offended by their inappropriateness. Passive behavior may range from psychotic denial, to seemingly innocent conflict avoidance, to compulsive (usually resentful) accommodation.

3) PASSIVE-AGGRESSIVENESS: The passive-aggressive person does not admit to or acknowledge their angry actions. They insist that their forget-fulness or misunderstandings or thoughtless statements are totally innocent and not intended to hurt or offend others. Instead of honestly acknowl-edging their anger, they find ways to hurt others without admitting their intentions.

4) CODEPENDENCE: Angry people often establish codependent rela-tionships. Because they have given up on working through the conflict, they adapt roles in hopes of limiting the damage to their feelings and their life that their offenders are creating (or that they are creating for them-selves). These relationships are too varied and complicated to be discussed in this format except to note that codependency is in fact sin—the sin of anger.

Codependent behavior may range from facilitating an addict (with roles as varied as the family's chronic overachiever, the family's clown, the family's designated black sheep, etc.) to rescuing others or becoming depressed.

But, is it really sin? Each of these relational patterns (the aggressive, the passive, the passive-aggressive, and the codependent) are anger-based strongholds for those who are legitimately being offended but are unable or unwilling to work through the dysfunctions productively. Hopefully, you can begin to see that even someone with the best seminary education, the deepest heart for God, and the most dedicated practice of their faith may never fully recognize their sin pattern (much less break free of it). Even though their sin may be unintentional and totally forgiven by God through His grace, it will continue to work destructive effects on their souls and the souls of others.

Sin can be very subtle and still be totally controlling. It is these subtle sin patterns that the performance-based Christian will have most difficulty seeing in herself. The grace-based Christian will eventually recognize how these subtle sins (described above) eat away at her heart and soul, and will go in search of the cause of it.

The Root Causes of Anger

The emotional root of anger is mistaking "sad" and "bad" for "mad."

Have you ever acted in anger when someone accidentally stepped on your toe, or spilled their milk, or misunderstood what you had said? These are examples of getting angry when no real offense has taken place. These are examples when the healthy emotional response would be sad, not mad.

I know a young man who is inhibited toward feeling sad. Therefore, when some sad thing happens he automatically has to reinterpret the event to require a mad, bad, or numb emotional response. He always reacts as if the sad event was someone's fault (if he decides the fault is with others, then he is mad; if he decides the fault is his, then he feels bad) or else it didn't really matter (numb). Since he is a very capable and confident person, he tends to blame others for the sad (nobody's fault) things in his life. The end result is that he tends to be an angry person. He has not learned how to respond to sad things as sad things (actually, he considers feeling sad to be a weakness).

This is just one example of how we may be conditioned to feel anger or respond with anger in circumstances where no one has truly offended us. I'm sure you can think of people you know who get angry without cause. We would be right in assuming that these people have psychological problems. Yet, these problems are also sin problems.

Learning the true nature and practice of forgiveness (see *Stickman Theology*, chapter 8) is essential for those who struggle with this type of anger problem. They may need the help of a counselor or patient friends to delve into their thinking and feeling to discover what other feelings they are inhibited to, whom they are legitimately angry with, what their expectations of themselves, others, and God really are. The negative situations they have yet to work through may no longer be external ones but ones from their past that they have internalized in an unhealthy way and now are not even aware they are being affected by.

THE RELATIONAL ROOT OF ANGER IS UNREALISTIC EXPECTATIONS.
I know a couple who are often angry with each other. Throughout their twenty years of marriage they have been faithful to each other, they have been sensitive toward each other, and they have worked hard to be good sexual, financial, and parenting partners. Yet, they consistently find reasons to be angry toward one another. He's mad that she moves too slow, she's mad that he likes jalapenos on almost all his food, etc. Things that they would not make issues of with anyone else, they expect the other to change. They have honestly believed that their love for one another entitles them to make demands upon each other that keep them at odds.

Once again, I offer an extreme example to illustrate a dynamic that we may all indulge in more subtle ways. Some of our expectations are so ingrained in us that they never really get examined. Yet, in a person without sinful anger, every expectation is open to discussion and modification. Even "biblical" expectations can be unrealistic. For instance, if your spouse is an introvert, they will probably never feel comfortable "evangelizing" strangers. This is no reflection on their spiritual depth or commitment. It is inappropriate for one person to continue to expect another to do something they have expressed (or shown) their objection to. To continue to be angry about these unmet expectations is sin.

When your expectations are not shared by others you are committed to it is appropriate to represent yourself, set your boundaries, and find alternative means of meeting those specific needs. It is not appropriate to continue expecting agreement and being upset when you do not get it.

THE SPIRITUAL ROOT OF ANGER IS MISINTERPRETING THE CHARACTER OF GOD.
Once upon a time a beautiful little girl was molested by her daddy. He was a preacher. Everyone seemed to think he was wonderful. Year after year he would abuse and molest her. When she was twelve her father left the ministry and his family to continue an affair. She had been used and cast away. He went on to marry another woman and have a good life. She was left to try to make sense of it all. You can imagine some of the conclusions she reached.

"God doesn't care about me." "God loves men more than women." "God knows that I deserved it." "God was trying to teach me something." "God's plan for my life is not to be trusted."

She felt insignificant and powerless. Her interpretations were totally understandable. Still, she was wrong. She desperately needed to get in touch with her anger in order to free herself from these consequences of her victimization.

The same applies to each of us. If we do not process our legitimate anger, we are left with no option but to misinterpret the character and purposes of God. Even when we ignore, dismiss, and minimize the wounds others inflict on us we are misinterpreting God's character and purposes. God does not ask us to be strong enough to suffer at the hands of others. No, He asks us be much stronger: He asks us to acknowledge our wounds and work through them in a healthy manner!

It may be helpful to explore one misinterpretation of God's character in particular. Since we are exploring our sin motivations, we are subject to some profound embarrassment for the sinful parts of our character that are being revealed. It would be a misinterpretation of God's character (a manifestation of sinful anger) to think that God is rejecting you for your sin. God does not condemn us (see Romans 8:1), but He does convict us. He wants us to embrace our healing and growth. If we withdraw from Him, it will not be because of His rejection of us, but of our rejection of Him.

Terry Ewing

The Cure for Anger: Patience

Let's take a closer look at the scripture verse quoted at the beginning of this chapter: "Dear brothers, take note of this: Everyone should be quick to listen, slow to speak, and slow to become angry, for man's anger does not bring about the righteous life that God desires" (James 1:19–20). There are four dynamics of patience listed in this verse: active listening, withholding a response, acknowledging your feelings, and embracing a relational goal.

1) BE QUICK TO LISTEN: Active listening is a spiritual discipline, and it is an act of patience. It is allowing for clarification, it is allowing for expression of feeling, and it is allowing for perspectives. Practicing active listening shows that you are trying hard to know and understand others. Active listeners ask "clarifying" questions, give eye contact, and even repeat back what they have heard. Being quick to listen suggests a true heart of respect for disagreements and honor of the differences with others (a healthy expectation indeed).

2) BE SLOW TO SPEAK: If we need someone to agree with us, we will have great difficulty being slow to speak. The patient person values understanding over agreement. When emotions become too strong, the patient person will call a time-out—stop the conversation with an agreement to pick it up later.

Those who are slow to speak do not avoid conflict; they embrace it as a necessary process. Patient people consider their words, but they don't deny their honest thoughts and feelings. In other words, give a thoughtful response; get control of yourself before you address the situation. Patient people offer respect and honor to others, but also expect the same from others.

3) BE SLOW TO BECOME ANGRY: Patient people have become patient by working through their past hurts productively. Then, when new situations occur, they are free to consider their feelings. They don't have the pressure of unprocessed past feelings waiting to explode into their present.

Patience is characterized by a life that is free to be present (aware of their own feelings, as well as the feelings of others). To be present should be considered a spiritual discipline on par with Bible study, scripture memory, accountability, etc.

4) BRING ABOUT THE RIGHTEOUS LIFE GOD DESIRES: What are your desires for your relationship with your spouse, children, friends, and family? Do you desire to know and be known at the deepest levels, to be accepted for who you are, to be trusted, to share a history of challenges, growth, learning, healing, and love? If so, keeping these goals in mind can work a miracle of patience in you.

These are passions that God wants to burn strong within you. Patience is not an absence of strong feelings; it is a passion all its own. A passion for godly relationships!

Small Group Discussion

1) Take five to ten minutes to rewrite Matthew 23:23–28 in terms that express appropriate anger toward someone who has wounded you. Share your rewrite with your group.

2) On a scale of one to ten (with one being very patient and ten being very angry) rate yourself. State why.

3) Who is the most patient person you know? What makes you think so?

4) Pray for each other's struggle against anger.

Chapter Eleven

Water Gun Duels with the Wicked Witch of the West

My oldest son, when he was seven to nine years old, watched the movie *The Wizard of Oz* at least a dozen times. You remember how scary the Wicked Witch of the West was. She had incredible powers. She could fly on her broom. She could throw fire. She had flying monkeys that attacked on her command. She even had an army of big tough guys, not to mention the field of poppies that could put you to sleep. Dorothy, the Scarecrow, the Tin Man, and the Lion had to steal her broom and bring the broom back to the Wizard of Oz in order to accomplish their purpose.

During the course of this adventure the "cowardly" Lion actually acts courageously, the Tin Man (without a heart) is very compassionate; and the Scarecrow (without a brain) comes up with a winning plan. They overcome their perceived weaknesses, but it is still not enough; the Wicked Witch is winning. And so, in the end, they are being chased all around until they are cornered by the witch's army. Then the Wicked Witch confronts them and proclaims that she is going to kill them all, one by one. When the witch sets the Scarecrow on fire, Dorothy picks up a nearby bucket of water and splashes the Scarecrow. Accidentally, some of the water lands on the witch, and the witch dissolves.

After watching this scene the first time I thought, "Well, why didn't they tell us at the first of the story that if you got the witch wet she would dissolve? It wouldn't have been nearly as scary." Think about it. Put yourself in the story. If I had been Dorothy and knew that the Wicked Witch could be melted away with water, I would have taken a set of water guns and challenged the Wicked Witch to a duel. I can imagine her flying down to the battleground, taking up her water gun, standing with me back to back, taking five paces, and then turning to fire. Maybe the Wicked Witch wins the duel, and I get wet: no big deal. But if I win, she dissolves away, or at least she loses some of her powers.

I believe we have that opportunity when we face our true enemies: Satan, our fallen world, negative peer pressure, and our own carnal nature. There are "water guns" that we can employ toward our own Wicked Witch of the West; these are the means of grace commonly referred to as spiritual disciplines.

We are given the task of confronting the power of our own Wicked Witches and stealing their brooms (embracing our trials, tribulations, and temptations as opportunities for healing and growth). We have all been beaten by our enemies at different times and in different ways; they are powerful. They have the ability to put us to sleep and to overwhelm us and to burn us up. And sometimes we are defenseless—literally. We are not going to win, because our enemies have established strongholds within us. Yet, we will never stop struggling to grow. We will never become content with our failures. Therefore, we must identify ways (relationally, spiritually, and emotionally) to dilute the power of these strongholds. One of the ways to dissolve the power of our strongholds is through exercising spiritual disciplines.

A spiritual discipline is a means of confronting our stronghold by utilizing weapons that are safe for us but deadly to our enemies. For example, if we commit to a three-day fast and after a day we eat, no sin has been committed, no harm has been done, you haven't lost, nor have you failed. You have offered your body and mind to God, and He has touched your soul. Maybe you didn't complete the challenge you set for yourself (your water gun duel with your Wicked Witch), but God is still delighted with your heart and your effort, win or lose.

However, when practicing spiritual disciplines, there is a way in which your spirit can be wounded. If you think of your exercise of a spiritual discipline as a legalistic standard by which you measure your own righteousness (or the righteousness of others) you turn your water gun duel into a true gunfight that you lose every time. Even if you accomplish the spiritual discipline you set for yourself, it is no longer a means of grace to you. Your spiritual discipline has become an exercise in pride, building your pride in self if you succeed and wounding your self-esteem if you fail. Either way, your spirit is wounded.

The practice of the spiritual disciplines must be understood as a means of opening ourselves to the grace of God. As we practice our spiritual disciplines, we should be continually calling upon God to strengthen us. We are not trying to prove ourselves or test others. We are actually availing ourselves of a means of grace. When practiced as a means of grace, the spiritual disciplines work like water on the Wicked Witch. Our dependence upon God developed during our practice of a spiritual discipline causes a profound weakening in the temptations we face thereafter.

THE DISCIPLINES WORK WITHIN US TO WEAKEN OUR STRONGHOLDS IN THREE WAYS:

1) Spiritual disciplines provide the Holy Spirit opportunity to establish healthy habits and to break unhealthy ones. This is simply the behavioral benefit—what we train ourselves to is what we get comfortable with, and it becomes our automatic response. In this way our relational root is strengthened. This is just our outward behavior: the way that we relate to people, the things that we incorporate into our lifestyle.

You may have wondered why this topic is presented as part of the relational root of our tree of righteousness. I believe that there is no other tool so effective in challenging our ability to relate to others in healthy ways as the practice of spiritual disciplines, even (maybe especially) if no one knows what you are doing.

There are many ways in which practicing spiritual disciplines enhances healthy relational patterns. I want to comment on three (you may be able to identify several others).

By challenging your strongholds through spiritual disciplines you are creating a personal challenge for yourself that is not based upon someone else (other than God) helping you or causing you to fail. You are breaking away from any unhealthy dependence on others. There are so many ways in which others can help or hurt you that sometimes it can seem as if others are more responsible for your success and failures than you are. Practicing spiritual disciplines creates a battleground on which you can reclaim for God and yourself the responsibility for your own decisions and attitudes.

Practicing spiritual disciplines strengthens your compassion toward the struggles of others. Even if you have never struggled with an addiction or been guilty of devastating moral failures, you can be much more compassionate toward the struggles of others when you have your own recent experiences of personal challenges that you have failed to complete (or know you would have failed to complete without the grace of God).

Spiritual disciplines provide a setting for you to practice healthy relationship patterns. For instance, when you are fasting you are not obligated to let anyone know what you are doing or why. Usually, someone will notice. Therefore, you will need to decide how much you want to tell. If someone knows that you are fasting, they can sympathize and be encouraging, but they can't do it for you. No one else should be obligated not to eat in front of you because you are fasting.

These are all healthy relational skills that some people never develop.

2) Spiritual disciplines are opportunities for the renewing of our minds. As we challenge ourselves to complete a discipline by seeking the grace of God, we are opening our minds to God in several ways:

We learn to recognize the presence of God! Wow! How many Christians go their whole lives never being able to separate the experience of God from their own emotions, imaginations, or intellectual beliefs? Some are left questioning whether they have ever really experienced God, whereas others end up claiming experiences of God that actually may not be.

We learn to recognize the power of God in us! Most Christians acknowledge miracles of healing and provision. We pray for those who are sick and those who are in need—as we should. However, I'm convinced that God exercises His power most freely in such intimate ways as calming our nerves, giving us insights into scripture, nudging our hearts toward acts of kindness, sharing our sorrows, etc.

Some may question if those activities really represent "power". How hard can they be? To answer that question, put yourself in the same situation. Which do you imagine would be easier for you to do if you had all the power? If you have all the power, is it easier to heal a body or comfort a heart? Which takes more wisdom, sensitivity, timing, understanding, and love? Practicing the spiritual disciplines renews our minds to seeking and appreciating all the power of God, especially the most intimate and difficult applications of His power.

We learn to recognize the purposes of God! Since God's purposes are evidenced in confessions of faith, repentance of sins, changed lives, saved marriages, ministries of evangelism and discipleship, acts of love, etc., we can tend to think that those results are God's purposes. Practicing the spiritual disciplines renews our minds to the primary purposes of God; enjoying us as we enjoy Him and healing us of anything and everything that inhibits that intimate relationship.

3)   Spiritual disciplines strengthen the influence of the Holy Spirit upon our innermost being, our spirits. This is the psychological benefit that strengthens our emotional root. In other words, this is where we are learning to trust the true nature of our hearts, understand ourselves, acknowledge our feelings, and to evaluate what is really happening within us.

Again, let's use fasting as an example. During the first day of a three-day fast I think I am really, really hungry. On day two, I'm hungrier. On day three I am weak. Next time I'm hungry, I have a scale of measurement to identify myself by. I learn how to evaluate what is happening within me. I start to be able to evaluate my strength level physically, my endurance level emotionally, and how to process these things relationally. These dynamics are the anchors of psychological health (since "psych" means "soul"). And, they are all natural products of practicing spiritual disciplines!

Setting Appropriate Goals

Usually the phrase "setting appropriate goals" implies that we should not commit to more than we can do and thereby set ourselves up for failure.

In practicing spiritual disciplines, just the opposite is true.

If your goal isn't beyond what you think you can accomplish (in and of yourself), then you probably are not exercising a spiritual discipline. You are exercising a physical discipline or an intellectual discipline. A spiritual discipline is a discipline that requires our dependence upon the power of the Holy Spirit within us. If your goal is to fast one meal, you will be exercising an intentional or a physical discipline. These disciplines have some value, but spiritual disciplines anticipate goals that are beyond our expectations of what we can accomplish. So we are stretching ourselves. Is it okay, in this one area, to set ourselves up to fail? Yes! Won't that get discouraging? No, because we have already established that failure is not detrimental to us. We don't have to protect ourselves from our failures anymore. There is so much understanding of ourselves and of God to be gained within this context of "safe failures."

Let's take a moment to detail some of the ways our water gun duels can be conducted.

Here are some ways to practice spiritual disciplines:

FASTING: Go without food. This is the most common way of fasting, but it may not be the way that challenges you most directly. You may also fast any unnecessary words. You may fast television or radio. You married couples may challenge yourselves by fasting sex (make it harder for yourselves by continuing to snuggle, kiss, and hug). Set your goal beyond any time limit you think you can accomplish in and of yourself. Call continuously upon God to strengthen you and give you joy in the effort.

SOLITUDE: Don't just get away from it all or escape the rat race, but get into the presence of God. Reflect upon your life. Have out-loud conversations with God. Get absorbed in the intricacies of His creation. Evaluate your relationships. Dream about God's plans for your future. Create new resolutions. I make resolutions every New Year. Usually I will write them out and share them with others. The ones with good memories may ask me, "Didn't you resolve to do some of those things last year and maybe the year before?" Well, yes. The fact that I didn't keep them doesn't mean that they weren't good things to commit to, so I commit to them again. "How many times will you commit to them?" As many times as it takes until I can incorporate the resolutions into my life. Someday I will incorporate them into my lifestyle. In the meantime, I will continue to make New Year's resolutions or birthday resolutions. It is a spiritual discipline. So my failure does not devalue the discipline at all.

MEMORIZING SCRIPTURE: Pick a chapter (or more) and live with it for as long as it takes to ingrain it into your soul and into your memory. Recite it to your spouse, your friends, your parents, and your children. Let the word of God grow in you richly.

If you don't mind, I would like to share with you one of the things I've learned about myself through the spiritual discipline of scripture memory. I have memorized chapters, numbers of chapters at a time, and then gone on to different chapters. That may sound impressive, but it really isn't. It is actually easier for me to memorize chapters than verses. The chapters have a context and flow that I can relate to better than individual verses. But, once I begin to memorize something different, I quickly forget what I previously memorized. I can't quote to you the chapters and chapters that I have memorized at different times, but the concepts stay with me. I feel connected with those who were the first recipients of each letter or book. I can forever identify those concepts, even though I might not even be able to tell you which chapter it was that I memorized once upon a time that I can't quote to you now.

Your practice of scripture memory may be very different from mine. We are not under an obligation to make it look any certain way. We want to give ourselves the freedom to let the spiritual disciplines grow us up.

WORSHIP: Worship, as a spiritual discipline, is stretching your emotional boundaries with God. If you are normally inclined to be introverted, then sing out loud, lift your hands, smile and laugh before God, be a little impulsive, and let yourself be embarrassed. Go ahead; be embarrassed. Stretch yourself. Let your love for Him be intimate and personal. If you are normally inclined to be extroverted, then calm down, be still, stand in humble reverence in awe of His majesty, let your love for Him be respectful.

ACCOUNTABILITY: Find someone with greater wisdom and a more mature love than your own and ask him or her to mentor you. Tell them what your weaknesses and failures are. Confess your sins. Share your hopes. Ask them to hold you to your new resolutions. Give them permission to pry into your life. Have them challenge you to practice other spiritual disciplines. Of course, developing such a relationship takes time. Be very careful whom you ask to take on this role in your life. If, after an appropriate period of time, the person you chose has not shared any of their own failures and weaknesses with you, then run from the relationship and don't look back.

Please remember that practicing accountability as a spiritual discipline is about holding each other to the convictions of our own hearts, individually. It is not about imposing a "higher" standard on someone than they desire for themselves.

JOURNALING: Don't limit God's voice to devotional thoughts. Assume that God is directing your life and speaking to you significantly. Anything that you think God is saying or doing is surely worth putting down on paper. Answered prayers, unanswered prayers, new principles you've learned, trials you are going through, the names of the people you are praying for, and every way that God blesses you are proper subjects for journaling.

PRAYER: Be honest with God. Tell Him what you truly feel, think, and hope. Then listen. Let Him tell you what He feels, thinks, and hopes. Don't be superficial with God, and don't do Him the favor of praying. He is jealous of your affections, and desires to communicate His love and caring for you.

SIMPLICITY: Develop a plan to reduce the time, energy, and money it takes to support your lifestyle. Brainstorm alternative lifestyles that facilitate greater amounts of your time, energy, and money be directed toward others. Don't be conformed to the pattern of this world!

OTHERS: Active listening to others, offering words of faith and praise to God, genuinely complimenting others, physical exercise—anything you can challenge yourself to with the expectation of God's help can be a spiritual discipline.

I once challenged a friend of mine to stop tithing and to save his tithe to pay for his daughter's wedding. I asked him to do this as a spiritual discipline. I knew that it would take more faith in God for him to not tithe than to tithe. His practice of tithing had become a religious ritual that he depended on to guarantee God's approval (as well as his own self-acceptance).

Are there right ways and wrong ways to practice a particular spiritual discipline? I don't think so. Again, go back to fasting. How do you fast correctly? Well, some will say fasting means taking nothing into your system except water. Some will say juices are allowed and advisable. Do whatever you do. For me, I will tell you, I will drink anything I can drink. Usually I will drink pop because it's got more sugar, more pick-me-up. And you say, "Well, you're not really fasting," and I'll say, "To heck I'm not; it's still a struggle. Don't tell me I'm not fasting."

Choosing your Spiritual Discipline

We have claimed spiritual disciplines as a means of grace, a context for safe failures, and as water gun duels with our Wicked Witches. As you have gone through this study of the Seven Deadly Sins you have been asked to identify the sin motivations that are most active in you. Now, instead of facing these sin motivations as they present themselves in the course of your life, you have a tool for facing these sin motivations in the context of spiritual disciplines.

Choose to practice a spiritual discipline that challenges you in the area of your most intense sin motivation.

IF YOU STRUGGLE WITH PRIDE: any spiritual discipline will do as long as you set a goal you know you can't accomplish.

IF YOU STRUGGLE WITH SLOTH: if you are mentally slothful, challenge yourself with a mental spiritual discipline (like scripture memory). If you are relationally slothful, challenge yourself with a relational spiritual discipline (like active listening, words of encouragement, or acts of kindness). If you are physically slothful, challenge yourself to a physical spiritual discipline (like cleaning your house or mowing your neighbor's yard).

IF YOU STRUGGLE WITH LUST: you might practice fasting in order to get comfortable with feelings of longing and compulsions; or practice looking for God in the eyes of those you lust after; or practice giving true compliments (affirming the Godly value) of everyone.

IF YOU STRUGGLE WITH GREED: explore the spiritual disciplines of simplicity, giving, and developing a relationship with someone who is financially destitute or struggling. Memorize chapters of Acts. Take a short-term missions trip.

IF YOU STRUGGLE WITH GLUTTONY: fasting your drug of choice and finding an accountability partner would be a direct challenge to the sin manifestation, but may not actually minister to the sin motivation. You may need a discipline that focuses on assuring you of your value and God's love. You may want to try immersing yourself in worship or Bible study.

IF YOU STRUGGLE WITH ENVY: you might practice seeing God through nature (an evidence of His love that applies to all people equally), practice meditating upon Jesus' sufferings on your behalf, or practice thanking God for each blessing you can identify in your life.

IF YOU STRUGGLE WITH ANGER: you may need to practice acknowledging your healthy feelings of anger, stating forgiveness toward those who have offended you, or praying for those who hurt you.

Every sin motivation should be confessed (acknowledged before men) and repented of (acknowledged before God). If you cannot confess your sin motivations before men you will be locked into them by secrecy (leading to shame or self-justification). These spiritual disciplines are not optional.

If you sugarcoat your sin motivations the first time you confess them, then try again, and again. Until you are comfortable acknowledging your sin motivations, the healing has not yet begun. So, take advantage of this study. Don't let this opportunity pass you by to embrace God's grace. When practiced as a means of grace, any spiritual discipline is an avenue for confrontation and healing for any sin motivation!

Small Group Discussion

1) If spiritual disciplines are truly meant as a means of grace, becoming legalistic in our practice of spiritual disciplines destroys their very purpose. Can you give an example of how you may have been legalistic in your practice of spiritual disciplines? Can you give an example of how your spiritual disciplines have been a means of grace to you?

2) Commit to your small group to practice one or more spiritual disciplines this week.

3) What benefit are you hoping to gain from the discipline you committed yourself to?

Chapter Twelve

Preparing Your Personal Narrative

Maybe you've heard the example given of how easy it is for us to misunderstand God's will for our lives. The example I have in mind is the characterization of the young man whose infatuation with the beautiful girl leads him to believe that God has directed him to marry the girl. It seems all too obvious that his wishes have played too big a role in his interpretations of God's direction for his life. However, we have to admit that we can't really know how God has directed another person. Certainly there are safeguards that can protect us from our misplaced enthusiasms, our ignorance, and our wishful thinking concerning God's will for our lives. We know that God's will for us will not violate the moral or theological truths revealed in the Bible; we know to value godly counsel; we know to anticipate a feeling of peace attending God's will. Still, there is room for so much confusion and diversity in how God directs us.

For instance, I happened to be one of those infatuated young men (thirty-some years ago) who believed God told him to marry the beautiful girl. I still believe it. I asked her, she said yes, and we got married shortly after I turned eighteen. I would not recommend that others marry so young, and I would be appropriately skeptical of those who claim God told them to. Yet, that is my story, and I'm stickin' to it!

This is just a small part of my personal narrative, or how I tell my own history from my own perspective. The Bible is full of such stories. We know about Mary's encounter with the angel that announced God's intention for her to be the mother of the messiah because she must have told her story.

The same is true for Zechariah's experience of God in the temple foretelling the birth of his son John (the Baptist). This is how the gospels begin, with people sharing their personal narratives. Jesus did the same. My favorite portion of Jesus' personal narrative is in Luke 4, which records the story of his strongest temptations.

I believe that it is important that each of us be very intentional about forming our own personal narratives. It is important to be able to tell yourself about yourself. How you think of yourself is very important to how you experience and deal with every event in your life. We all have this storyline developing in our thoughts, but it still takes very intentional effort to say those thoughts out loud and evaluate them among safe people. Without stating our narratives out loud, our storylines can take on a life of their own that is empowered by our sin motivations.

In this chapter I want to challenge you to develop your personal narrative. What have been the most significant people and events in your life? How have they shaped you? How has God impacted your life? What have been your greatest temptations, your greatest successes, your greatest hopes and dreams, your greatest failures? How do these things still affect you? What kind of family were you raised in? Is your temperament more like your mom's or your dad's? What are your wounds? Whom have you wounded? What are your spiritual gifts? Do you have a vision from God for your life? These are questions that create a grid through which you interpret the events of your day-to-day living. How you answer these questions contributes very powerfully to your sin motivations or your passions for godliness.

Take, for instance, the following question: Why did you yell at your child? Answer: Because she made me angry. Within this storyline is a personal narrative. It includes a belief that your child has the power to make you yell. You are a victim to your child. Her behavior can control yours.

Too many people will never evaluate the story they are telling themselves in situations like this. They may very sincerely tell themselves that they shouldn't be yelling at their child, yet never realize why the storyline they are believing is empowering a behavior they wish to change.

Embracing Your Personal Narrative

I remember counseling with a gentleman who thought his wife might be crazy. The stories he told about her certainly made her sound crazy to me. I asked if she would be willing to come with him to his counseling sessions. It didn't take long for me to be able to affirm that his wife did indeed have a psychological illness. I told the two of them my diagnosis, and they calmly admitted that two psychologists they had seen in the past had reached the same conclusion. Then the wife explained that in each case the husband had "set the stage" before inviting her to visit with the counselors. She was convinced that her husband was manipulating the situation (part of her illness). She was not at all willing to entertain the possibility that her perceptions and actions were dysfunctional.

I continued to meet with the husband, who had every reason to think his wife was ill, but who continued to feel badly about painting her in a bad light. He had an emotional inhibition against embracing the reality of his wife's illness. We eventually discovered that he had been conditioned since childhood to feel bad about himself. He could not accept the praise and admiration that his previous counselors and I claimed he deserved for the remarkable coping mechanisms and life-facilitating dynamics he had incorporated into his marriage to such an ill person. He felt guilty for "manipulating" her in the many ways he had to in order to limit her destructiveness and facilitate her areas of productive functioning. He could not see his "manipulations" as wise and loving ministry. As far as I know, he continues to function in his marriage by "doing what he has to do" while feeling guilty about it. My prayer is that as his wife's condition deteriorates he be able to embrace the reality of her illness before his own depression becomes suicidal.

When Your Strengths Become Your Weaknesses

The story above is an extreme example of someone unable to embrace his personal narrative. He has come to trust in his "humility" to maintain his functioning. He learned to embrace his poor self-esteem in childhood in order to be acceptable to his parents (who loved to think of themselves as martyrs for the kingdom). He was taught that he was a burden to them and he should appreciate the sacrifices they made on his behalf. As an adult he was able to give a very thoughtful personal narrative that was confirmed by every clinical skill I possessed, yet he couldn't embrace it emotionally. Therefore, he was never able to forgive his parents, his wife, and others for their offences against him, because he didn't allow himself to be offended. In his mind his humility was his redeeming quality, instead of the life-killing self-debasement I see it to be.

You see, as a child, he had developed a way of giving his parents the appreciation they so desperately wanted by "humbling" himself. As a child, this was truly a remarkable coping mechanism that led to him being very accepted by other authority figures, primarily schoolteachers and church leaders. He was often described as "the perfect child," "the perfect student," "a youth director's dream," etc. He conformed to the expectations of everyone around him, and it served him well. His humility was a strength that he depended upon: it defined him. He trusted his humility and couldn't see himself acting in any other way. And yet, it is killing him. His humility locks him into a distorted self-perception that steals the joy and encouragement God has for him and may very well empower his suicidal ideations until he finally totally self-destructs.

His greatest strength is also his greatest weakness.

Possibly, this was also the case with King Solomon. I have often wondered how the wisest man that ever lived could end up embracing a gluttony toward his wives and concubines that led him to betray God. After all, wisdom is the opposite of gluttony. Yet, it seems that Solomon's great strength (wisdom) was twisted to become his greatest weakness (gluttony). His fall is described this way:

> King Solomon, however, loved many foreign women besides Pharaoh's daughter—Moabites, Ammonites, Edomites, Sidonians and Hittites. They were from nations about which the Lord had told the Israelites, "You must not intermarry with them, because they will surely turn your hearts after their gods." Nevertheless, Solomon held fast to them in love. He had seven hundred wives of royal birth and three hundred concu-

bines, and his wives led him astray. As Solomon grew old, his wives turned his heart after other gods, and his heart was not fully devoted to the Lord his God, as the heart of David his father had been. He followed Ashtoreth the goddess of the Sidonians, and Molech the destestable god of the Ammonites.

1 Kings 11:1–5

Biblical scholars can explain how the taking of so many wives and concubines, as well as the gods of their culture, could be a wise thing for a ruler of that time to do. It seems that this practice served many social and political purposes. It appears that Solomon did not question his own wisdom in this regard. He trusted his wisdom above the directives of God. And, in the end, he betrayed God, who had given him his gift of wisdom. The wisest person who ever lived somehow lost track of his own story. He got caught up in himself and, therefore, became unaware that his strength had become his weakness.

Forgetting All the Lord Has Done for Us

The Old Testament is full of examples of this principle. The most prominent may be the repeated cycle of Israel's deliverances by the judges. Time and again God would bless His people, then His people would be satisfied with their lives and "forget all that the Lord had done for them." Soon they would fall into idolatry, God would withdraw His blessings and protection, and they would find themselves "crying out to the Lord their God." God would raise up a judge to deliver them. He would bless their lives until they once again became satisfied and "forgot all that the Lord had done for them."

This is such a compelling pattern for you and me. My wife and I saw the movie *The Pursuit of Happyness*. The movie depicts a man who was very intelligent, worked very hard, and had a great attitude toward people and life. Yet, he was failing in his efforts to provide for his family. His wife finally leaves him, and he suffers great hardships trying desperately to provide for his son while risking failure again in an ambitious and risky stockbroker intern program. In the end, the father succeeds and eventually becomes a millionaire.

So, was the story about how money brings happiness? No, it was about how desperately we need to be known for who we are. The character in the movie needed to be known as a man who loved his family. An intelligent man. A diligent man. A capable man. The movie is the story of how he finally proved himself to himself.

Such a success story isn't promised to each of us, but we are promised that we are known and loved for who we are. This is the kind of "happyness" the movie was about. It is also the kind of "happyness" God has been working all your life to provide for you. This is the story only you can tell. It is a story that every Christian could honestly tell. But, do you know this story? Do you remember the times that God has met you at your points of need, or directed your steps, or forgiven your sins, or given you the strength to make a stand, or shown you His love in a way specially designed to heal your heart?

I want to challenge you to put that story on paper. Tell the story of you. Tell us who you are and how you got this way! Your story is too valuable to be forgotten!

Sharing Your Personal Narrative

If you have gone through this course of study with a small group, then you will know by now if your group can be trusted to hear your story. If you feel like you have to tell your story in a certain way, protect your parents, hide your failures, keep certain feelings to yourself, then don't tell your story at all. If you tell it the way someone else needs to hear it, then it is not really your story, is it?

It would be better to simply tell your group the truth. The truth may be:

1) I don't really know how to tell my story yet, or
2) I'm not confident that it is safe to share my story with you yet, or
3) I'm ashamed of my story, and I don't want to tell it yet, or
4) I don't really believe telling our stories is what Christians are supposed to do, or
5) Other.

Or, maybe you are ready to tell your story. You may be ready for people to hear what you tell yourself about yourself. You may be ready for some others to start to really know you from the inside out. You may really need others to question some of the ways you have told your story. If so, then go for it. Risk yourself.

Work with your personal narrative until you can share it in twenty minutes or less. This way you will not have time to defend or explain your story, only to tell it. Don't try to work in the details that would convince others that the way you are telling your story is the right way. Just tell the story.

Once you have spoken your personal narrative there may be themes that no longer seem quite right to you. Let yourself clarify your story as you live with it. This is one of the goals of sharing your story. Let your perspective of yourself grow and develop. Don't take your story as gospel; just let it be an honest disclosure of what you know about yourself today!

A final reminder: You don't know someone until you know their weaknesses.

If you have gone through this course of study with a small group you have already shared very deeply. I hope you have been shown love and acceptance. I hope you have come to see yourself as a member of a struggling, striving, growing family of faith.

If you have studied this book individually, please know that the information in this book is valuable only to the extent that it enables you to know yourself and share your struggling, striving, and growing with others. Don't give up until you find safe people to share yourself with, and, if you can't find them, challenge some people to become safe. Invite them to study and apply *Stickman Theology* and *Stickman's Battles* with you in a small group context or as a soul-care partner. Or, better yet, apply the principles you have learned and practiced during the course of this study to whatever curriculums or books or sermons or lessons you come across next. Just be a stickman and let others think of you whatever they will. Some will be drawn to you, some will be put off by you—kind of the same way people related to Jesus.

Be yourself! Don't go around trying to be the best you can be. Be who you are while fully expecting the Holy Spirit to continue His work of healing and growth in you. If you find that others can't love you for who you are, then you can be assured that they are equally incapable of loving themselves for who they are. Meanwhile, love them anyway. Pray for their healing and growth. Set the true standard of Christ: honesty, transparency, faith, hope, and love.